THE BETTER ENTREPRENEUR

The Better Entrepreneur

Unlock Balance to Lead Better, Grow Faster, and Profit More

JT Wiederholt, MPAS™, CFP®, CEPA®, APMA®

Published by Game Changer Publishing

Paperback ISBN: 978-1-969372-86-5

Hardcover ISBN: 978-1-969372-85-8

Digital ISBN: 978-1-969372-87-2

www.GameChangerPublishing.com

PRAISE FOR "THE BETTER ENTREPRENEUR"

"'The Better Entrepreneur' is more than a guidebook—it's a reflection of JT Wiederholt's lived experience and leadership. I've known JT for over fifteen years and have partnered with him on numerous endeavors. He's not only written about the entrepreneurial journey, but he's also lived it, wearing the many hats he references with authenticity and grit. In a time when the financial services industry is evolving faster than ever, leadership will be the defining factor between those who adapt and those who fall behind. JT understands these matters deeply. His insights are grounded in real-world experience and a genuine commitment to helping others succeed. As a trusted advisor to many financial professionals, JT brings clarity, strategy, and heart to every conversation, and this book is no exception. If you're serious about leading in a fast-changing environment, this book belongs on your desk, not your shelf."

—Michael E. Lawson
Regional Vice President

"JT has been one of the most effective coaches I have worked with throughout my tenure in senior leadership. His knowledge, expertise, and communication style when it comes to leading and supporting small business owners, has been incredibly impactful and well-received with our growing network of long-tenured and successful advisors."

—Thomas North, CFP®, ChFC®, CFS®
Franchise Regional VP

"JT Wiederholt is one of the most experienced business minds I've had the privilege to learn from. His understanding of both the corporate landscape and practical, real-world business execution makes him a rare and valuable resource. Over the years, I've gained tremendous knowledge from JT with his strategic thinking, clarity, and ability to distill complex ideas into actionable insights. He consistently demonstrates unparalleled skills in listening, advising, and guiding sound business decisions. I'm thrilled he's chosen to share his expertise more broadly through this book."

—Britt Tappen
Sr. Franchise Field Vice President

"JT possesses a spectacular combination of head and heart leadership—understanding the importance of systems and structure to one's success, but perhaps more importantly, understanding the need to build and maintain an incredible culture. He has helped countless entrepreneurs and leaders tap into the ideal balance of these two ideas. 'The Better Entrepreneur' is a must-read for anyone striving to achieve substantial growth while building an organization that people are knocking down the door to be a part of."

—Brian J. Mora, CFP®, CRPC®, AWMA®
Senior Vice President—Head of
Experienced Advisor Recruiting

"During a transition, JT provided a calming, strong leadership presence. He guided me in developing a strong team and a focus for the practice's future. His strategies, recommendations, and tools were key components in the foundation for my practice. We continue to grow due to his guidance."

—Jennifer Marcontell, CFP®, BFA™,
ChFC®, AAMS®, APMA®, CRPC®
Barron's Hall of Fame Advisor

READ THIS FIRST

Just to say thanks for buying and reading my book,
I would like to give you some great free tools, assessments,
and resources to enrich your entrepreneurial journey,
no strings attached!

DEDICATION

As a man of faith, I dedicate all that I do and have to my God. The greatest gift that I cherish, granted by my Heavenly Father, is the agency to act and react in the manner I choose to the experiences and circumstances of this life. My greatest decision was to enter into a union with a choice woman and build a family together. Family is everything. This book could not have been possible without the constant companionship, support, forgiveness, and patience of my dear wife, Kim. She is tenacious and a constant seeker of truth. Where I am weak, she is unwavering. Kim has allowed me the countless hours of work and dedication necessary to hone my keen understanding and ability to assist, mold, and lead the entrepreneurs I work with to achieve their best purpose.

Our children have given up time with Dad at times in this pursuit of excellence as well. Elijah is our family rock—he is steady in his faith and is authentic in everything he does. Jill is the second mother of our family—her presence is always calming, and her joy for life makes everyone lighter. Hyrum has a tender heart and a sharp mind—the combination that makes for an incredible friend and advocate. Eve is our energizer bunny—she is the life of the party and is dialed to a 10 in her empathy. How many people do you know that will fast for a homeless man they've seen once? Kate is wise beyond her years, and I expect to see a few good books written by her in the future; she fights for truth and sees what others don't see. Although our youngest didn't make it, Moses is our family's light bearer in the hope for a better world beyond this mortal life. This book is dedicated to my family.

I have a tribe beyond my family, too! My sister Keli was my ride or die in my childhood and a woman of conviction and faith in our adulthood. My mom and dad are the people who formed my view of the world as a child and made incredibly powerful personal changes so that I could live a better life. I have been blessed with grandparents, great aunts and uncles, and in-laws that I adore and respect. Professionally, Shaun Scott and Ali Stucky are my left and right hands. They are the ones on whom I rely to make our coaching business what it is today. Mark and Dave are my partners in wealth management and have incredible minds for running a disciplined and profitable business. These professional partners are friends, and their dedication to creating something truly special brings great satisfaction to my day-to-day life.

The human family is glorious, and the people I've had the privilege to associate with, learn from, and do business with echo in the annals of my personal history. May you, as the reader, see the threads of this tapestry of experience with all of these influential people and appreciate them as much as I do. Thanks for reading!

THE BETTER ENTREPRENEUR

UNLOCK BALANCE TO LEAD BETTER,
GROW FASTER, AND PROFIT MORE

JT WIEDERHOLT

FOREWORD

BY BILL WILLIAMS

After almost four decades of working in financial services for a nationally recognized brand and leading a variety of businesses all focused on providing a superior client experience in an ultra-competitive industry, I have come to understand that success requires a plan that includes the following essential ingredients: a defined WHY, the right people, a repeatable process to deliver value, and a P&L that has consistent P.

JT, having worked as a leader in multiple areas of my business, has truly captured these elements with clarity, stories, and actionable steps for success. He is a master of his craft and a superior coach.

Purpose is the starting point for every entrepreneur's journey. In the opening chapter, JT challenges readers to reconnect with their core motivations, asking, "What is your purpose, cause, or passion?" He makes it clear that the trajectory of a business is inseparable from the clarity of its leader's vision. The section "Your Reawakening" is not just a call to introspection—it is a blueprint for aligning personal values with organizational goals. JT's assertion that "as you go, so goes your business" is a powerful reminder that leadership begins with self-awareness.

People are the heart of any enterprise, but JT reframes the traditional view of management. In "Leadership Matters," he argues that the better entrepreneur manages systems, not people. This shift from direct oversight to ecosystem-building is essential for sustainable growth. Drawing on his experience leading corporate teams and advising entrepreneurs, JT provides practical guidance on cultivating environments where individuals and systems work in harmony. The concept of an "ECOsystem" is particularly relevant for leaders seeking to foster collaboration and resilience.

Process is the engine that drives culture. JT's chapter on process emphasizes that discipline is not merely a matter of routine but of intentional rituals that shape organizational behavior. "Your culture lives and dies by process," he writes, urging leaders to evaluate whether their rituals are building or undermining their desired culture. This perspective is informed by JT's work with franchise systems, where process discipline is often the differentiator between success and stagnation. The idea that "discipline comes from disciple" challenges readers to consider the deeper purpose behind their operational routines.

Profit is addressed with equal rigor. JT reminds readers that "what gets measured gets done," advocating for a data-driven approach to performance management. He explores the balance between speed and sustainability, noting, "If you want to go fast, go alone; if you want to go far, go together." This principle is particularly relevant for leaders seeking to align their teams around shared objectives and transparent metrics. JT's experience in helping entrepreneurs and advisors clarify what is important—and communicate that effectively to their teams—comes through in this section.

Potential is the culmination of the entrepreneurial journey. JT introduces the concept of building either a prison or a path, challenging readers to consider whether their current trajectory is limiting or liberating. The three stages—Better Team, Better Business, and Better Freedom—provide a roadmap for unlocking latent potential and achieving long-term success. JT's approach encourages leaders to continually assess where their greatest opportunities lie and to commit to ongoing growth.

PRACTICAL APPLICATION AND STRATEGIC INSIGHT

Throughout the book, JT's approach is both analytical and actionable. He draws on his experience as a consultant and leader to offer strategies that are immediately applicable, whether the reader is an advisor, entrepreneur, or corporate executive. The emphasis on systems, measurement, and disciplined execution reflects JT's belief that sustainable growth is the result of intentional design, not happenstance.

The closing section, "Putting It All Together: What's Your Better?" challenges readers to synthesize the principles and commit to a path of continuous improvement. JT's assertion that "clarity brings commitment and action" is a call to move beyond aspiration and toward measurable progress.

WHY THIS BOOK MATTERS

The value of "The Better Entrepreneur" lies in its clarity and relevance. JT's framework is adaptable to organizations of all sizes and industries, making it a vital resource for leaders navigating change and seeking to build resilient, high-performing teams. The book's structure encourages reflection and self-assessment, while its practical tools enable immediate implementation.

Having worked alongside JT and witnessed his impact on advisors and entrepreneurs, I can attest to the effectiveness of his methods. His work has consistently helped business owners achieve growth that is both profitable and sustainable. JT's reputation as a top franchise consultant is well-earned, and his insights into leveraging technology and leadership systems are particularly valuable in today's competitive environment.

The Better Entrepreneur is more than a guide—it is a strategic resource for those committed to excellence. JT's 5 Principles are grounded in experience and validated by results. Readers will find in these pages a roadmap for unlocking balance, leading with purpose, and achieving growth that endures.

As you engage with this book, I encourage you to approach it not just as a source of ideas but as a catalyst for action. The journey to becoming a better entrepreneur begins with clarity, discipline, and a willingness to embrace change. JT's framework provides the tools; the commitment to apply them is yours.

—*Bill Williams*
Executive Vice President,
Ameriprise Franchise Group and
Ameriprise Advisor Center
Ameriprise Financial, LLC

FOREWORD

BY DOUG LENNICK

For those of us interested in creating something for the world that its people need, or for those of us interested in taking something that people are already benefiting from and improving it, JT Wiederholt has written this book. This book is written *for* me and *to* me, and *The Better Entrepreneur: Unlock Balance to Lead Better, Grow Faster, and Profit More* is written *for* you and *to* you as well.

I happen to be one of those people who believes that there is no end to better, and because that is true, JT "had me at the title."

The Better Entrepreneur. Whether you are a longtime entrepreneur like me, or a fresh-out-of-the-block entrepreneur, or someone considering the big question, "To be or not to be?," you will find wisdom ranging from the philosophical to the practical.

When my son Alan Lennick made the entrepreneurial leap into the business of financial advice, I shared with him that success would necessitate that two things be true: one, that he have passion for the value his business would provide to its clients; and two, that the foundation for growing his business would be retention of his clients and that client retention only happens on a bedrock of integrity.

In the year 1776, the United States of America was born, and Scottish moral philosopher Adam Smith's game-changing book *The Wealth of Nations* was published. Adam Smith, as I interpreted him, essentially stated that a capitalist could only be considered an "enlightened capitalist" if he or she acted in the best interest of their customers. JT Wiederholt is enlightened, and he believes that too. In *The Better Entrepreneur,* he shares with all of us *how* and *why* he brings that to his life and his business.

JT Wiederholt is a principle-based leader (the late, great leadership philosopher, author, and businessperson Stephen R. Covey would have been proud), and he identifies 5 Principles for entrepreneurs to "Unlock Balance to Lead Better, Grow Faster, and Profit More."

Five principles. 5 P's.

- Purpose
- People
- Process
- Profit
- Potential

Bestselling author Richard Leider, who himself studied under Victor Frankl in the late 1960s, understands and writes about "The Power of Purpose" in his book of that title.

JT notes that entrepreneurs are purpose-driven people. As JT puts it in the first chapter, "Entrepreneurship is a calling... For many, the necessity is to improve their lot in life in the form of economics and cash flow. Others are compelled to build a business because of a unique creation or skill set they know will better the world and the people around them."

Four questions stare at the entrepreneur:

1. What am I going to bring to the market that the world will benefit from?
2. How am I going to do it?
3. Why am I doing it?
4. Who, if anyone else, am I doing it with?

Purpose and people, the first two principles, are all about *why* and *who. Why* and *who* are the two most important questions.

Process and profit are all about *what* and *how.*

Potential is *what is being realized* on the journey.

The purpose of business is no more to make money than the purpose of life is to breathe. That said, absent breathing, there is no life, and absent profit, there is no business. And with profit comes more opportunities to make an even bigger difference.

You are reading this book because you have a purpose. You have more to give this world, and you know it. You also know that it is time to take the leap or time to get better at the leap you've already taken. Knowing. Deciding. What's next? Doing is what's next!

—*Doug Lennick*
CEO & Co-Founder
Think2Perform

CONTENTS

INTRODUCTION

I'd describe myself as just a normal guy. Everyone is unique, of course, and I've come to admire and appreciate the people I've come across in my life for all of their talents and flaws. In that sense, I'm just the same as you, the reader, and the other people you know.

One thing that is unique to me is my marriage of twenty-eight years to my wonderful wife, Kim, and our six children, one of whom is in heaven. I'm a partner in a thriving small business, the founder of our coaching business, an avid reader, and have traveled consistently over the past fifteen years, including having been to all fifty of the United States and over seventy countries and counting.

I've started a small business that failed miserably. I've also founded a business that is alive and growing rapidly. My most important accomplishment thus far is the perpetuation of my and Kim's legacy through who our children are and who they will become. In the end, what will be left of me after I've left this mortal life will echo in my children and their children.

Success in this life is measured in many ways. To me, the most important metric is the development of talents, spiritual growth, emotional competency, and the kindness my namesakes bless this world with.

My early story is one of grit, divine providence, and parents who cared more about me than themselves. I am a product of my parents' decisions and have attempted to honor their intentions and choices on my and my sister's behalf. My early years, like many, began with some disadvantages and some advantages.

For advantages, I consider being born in a part of the world where I've been afforded the freedom and opportunities to pursue a quality education, surrounded for the most part by safety and order in the people and government around me. I also attribute the idea of exploring the entrepreneurial journey (and perhaps also the courage to do so) to my late step-grandfather, Jack.

Jack came into my life at an early age and was always someone I admired and looked up to. He was a man not only large in stature but also a fantastic storyteller. Grandpa Jack was simply larger than life for me as a child and young man. In his early career, Jack worked for a small firm and learned his craft through a team of professionals. Although I don't know the details of his journey, the broad strokes are fairly similar to my own, and I'm grateful to have followed his model.

Jack was a land appraiser in the great state of Montana, USA. His business was unique, specialized, and built on reputation and results. He was an incredible networker and had "the gift of gab." He loved to spend time at a local diner in the mornings, swapping stories with longtime professional and personal friends. He acted as a key witness during land and other disputes and carried himself with confidence and ease in nearly any situation he found himself in.

As a child, I recall coming downstairs and hearing him providing counsel over the phone or typing up detailed reports on large land deals he was a part of. I loved the story he would tell, when I asked, about his encounter with the famed late-night talk show host of the '90s, David Letterman. Jack's observation was that Letterman, while witty and playful on TV, had none of those qualities when conducting business. He was a true straight man and not much for small talk.

Jack had dealings with others of the elite class and never seemed to be star-struck. He wasn't impressed by celebrity, fame, or money. Jack had an even keel about himself that seemed to have rubbed off on me: cool, calm, and collected, never too high and never too low. This also impacted how his business operated.

In my experience, until an entrepreneurial venture turns into an enterprise model, the business *is* the founder. As the founder goes, so goes the business. This is true in behavior, finances, and execution. The founder's reality is the business's reality; the quality of experience and delivery of products or services all reflect the warmth or coolness of the owner. (This is a topic we'll explore further in the first chapter, Principle 1: Purpose.)

In all practicality, there is a reason people refer to the business as their "baby." Just as we are a product of the parents and environment we grew up in, so is a business a product of the life experience, mindset, and personality of the founder. In that way, I got to where I am today based on the people, environment, and choices I've made along the way.

There's a formula to it all that we will explore together soon. My business today, like yours, reflects the culmination of my own experiences along the way.

It's been said that everyone has at least one good book in them. I'm hoping that I have more to give. My purpose for writing this book is built on the idea that entrepreneurialism is a lonely gig, and I want to take any chance I have to encourage those on this path to carry on. I feel like it is my duty to do so. I am fascinated by the uniqueness of each founder's story and the unspoken obstacles, challenges, and difficulties they've faced to achieve what they have.

In my day-to-day coaching and consulting work, I have presented hundreds of times and had thousands of conversations with owners of small businesses who've confided in me about the incredibly difficult situations they've faced. This is especially true in the early years of building a business: not knowing where the next new customer or client will come from, wondering if there will be enough money at the end of the month to cover personal or family needs, questioning whether borrowing is necessary, or even having to put payroll on a credit card. The list seems almost infinite in terms of the major and minor challenges an entrepreneur faces.

So, this book is a calling for me to encourage and support the entrepreneurs who feel like they're the only ones. To show that these are shared experiences and that, even though each business is unique, we all have commonalities that can be organized into principles that provide meaning and context to the problems faced. I am compelled to bring these concepts together in one place to provide support and coaching and to honor the legacy of those who've gone before, including my Grandpa Jack. The journey, while incredibly difficult, is worth it.

This book is for the entrepreneur. It's in the title, and the entrepreneurial fingerprint is on every page. While the phrasing may seem focused on the founder or initial developer of a business, the principles outlined in this book will benefit and support any member of the ownership or executive team leading the business. This book can be of tremendous help to any member of the team who is building the business and looking for help in organizing and compartmentalizing the issues and challenges they face.

In my coaching experience, I've found that there are 5 Principles that come together to provide a relative framework for the implementation and execution of a better business. To be a better entrepreneur, one will be well-served to leverage these 5 Principles as they work in the business daily and on the company in their strategic sessions. Contemplation and action can come together in a powerful way for the entrepreneur who is trying to take their business to the next level.

Journalist and author Malcolm Gladwell, in his book *Outliers*, concluded that 10,000 hours of practice are necessary to achieve mastery in a particular skill. With as much research as went into Gladwell's findings, I've reached a similar perspective. In the work I've done with professionals in different industries, I can quickly get a sense of whether I'm in front of someone who's on their way to or has surpassed the 10,000-hour mark.

In my twenty-five-plus years of leadership, management, consulting, and coaching, I've had the benefit of surpassing the 10,000-hour marker of coaching, mentoring, and consulting in a number of areas. This level of achievement is referred to as "unconscious competence." You may have this in your own area of expertise. It's encapsulated by the phrase, "You've forgotten more about a subject than the person in front of you knows." This level of confidence isn't boasting; it's simply the result of getting up after falling over and over again while learning along the way.

Personally, I've started a business and failed miserably. I've been mentored and trained by people who've achieved unconscious competence. I've been blessed with incredible partners who have served as sounding boards and litmus tests for ideas and decisions. Through these experiences, I have achieved a level of expertise that gives me great confidence that the reader of this book will benefit significantly as they seek to be better.

Most of the clients my team and I have worked with have experienced quantum growth in their businesses. Some desired to achieve topline revenue goals, others focused on profitability and bottom-line results, while still others were looking to unlock greater time and freedom for themselves. In my experience, an entrepreneur goes through a journey from building a team to building a business to unlocking greater freedom from the business. No matter where one may find themselves along the journey, goal achievement must be clearly defined to suit the owner. Growth for growth's sake is a fool's errand. What can feel like progress can actually be the building blocks of a prison. When the business runs you, a lack of freedom and autonomy becomes a self-made trap.

In addition to my success in helping hundreds of businesses and thousands of professionals, I've sought to deepen my understanding of the entrepreneur's journey with additional professional designations in disciplines of study that have created a strong foundation for me, including a Six Sigma Black Belt and CEPA® (Certified Exit Planning Adviser). These designations, along with a Master's in Financial Planning™ and CFP® (Certified Financial Planner), bring a rich combination of practical experience and educational discipline.

My hope is that the content of this book speaks for itself and that the practical actions you'll be able to take as a result of what you learn will be worth the price of admission.

As you learn more about each of the 5 Principles outlined in each chapter, you will find actionable steps you can take at the end of each one. The QR code in the front and back of the book will take you to online tools and further information to help you deepen your ability to execute the 5 Principles in your business.

I've found that most entrepreneurs succeed in their business through determination, dedication, grit, and countless hours of hard work. They are seeking a way to do what they do with greater efficiency and efficacy. Entrepreneurs can expand their margins, drive additional sales, create a better culture, design and implement systems, and develop the next generation of leaders in their business by following the outlined principles. Most great business owners I've met and worked with have unlocked components of the 5 Principles, but not all. If one hasn't implemented all of them fully, it is likely due to a lack of awareness, time, or competency. By reading this book and implementing its recommendations, you'll get closer than ever to your goals.

Because each reader is entering the 5 Principles from a different vantage point and experience, the formula for success will be unique to you. It is up to you to be clear on what you need from the 5 Principles and the steps to take to achieve your own success.

As we turn to the 5 Principles, it is important to recognize that, while the entrepreneur's path is a lonely one, it is almost never completed alone. For one to gain maximum value from the 5 Principles, leadership of a team is a foregone conclusion. The transferability of a one-man or one-woman business simply isn't there—I'm speaking of the salability or replication of what makes that individual marketable. The business *is* the individual, and everything it produces is based upon the individual's abilities, capacity, or content.

If your business is in entertainment, authorship, content creation, or intellectual capital that can perpetuate long after you're gone, then my statement may be wrong. Think of the royalties from music created by Michael Jackson or book sales of authors who have long passed. This can be a perpetual benefit to the next owner of the rights to these works. Perhaps this book isn't for this kind of entrepreneur? The more I think of it, however, there are people employed even in these cases: agents, assistants, producers, and the list goes on. My point is that the entrepreneur's experience is almost always surrounded by people, but this doesn't change the fact that it can feel extremely lonely. Even in that loneliness, the entrepreneur must rely upon others to achieve the end goal of their business. Effective leadership of those upon whom the entrepreneur is reliant is an imperative.

Author and management guru Peter Drucker has been quoted as saying, "Execution eats strategy for breakfast." In my experience, the difference between an entrepreneur who is able to continue to drive their business to the next level and one who is not, in its simplest terms, is execution. My hope for you as the reader is that you'll be able to connect with how each of the 5 Principles can make you a better owner and entrepreneur, but more importantly, that you're able to unlock their value through consistent implementation of the recommended action items I'll outline to maximize results.

There is certainly value in reading and understanding what each of the 5 Principles can do for you. However, my hope is that you're able to unlock that next level of greatness in yourself and in your business. The path to do so requires action. *It is in the doing that we become.* May you fulfill all of your potential!

PRINCIPLE 1: PURPOSE

Entrepreneurship is a calling.

For some, it may have come out of necessity. In my travels around the world, I've admired hardworking small business owners from all walks of life. I've seen a simple street vendor take immense pride in their product and take incredible care to serve a customer they may never meet again. I was humbled to witness the hustle and tenacity of a young boy on the streets of India who wouldn't take no for an answer. Even when I simply wanted to reward his persistence with an offer of change for no prize, his sense of integrity wouldn't allow him to accept the charity without providing his product in return.

For many, the necessity is to improve their lot in life in the form of economics and cash flow. Others are compelled to build a business because of a unique creation or skill set they know will better the world and the people around them. Whatever the motivation, you know when you've been called, and it is quite a compelling experience!

While the calling may be compelling, the better entrepreneur seeks to qualify themselves to successfully answer the call—that *qualifying* has everything to do with knowing oneself and the mastery needed to become, well, *better*! Personally, I find that the skill we're about to cover together, if it isn't the most important, is certainly on the shortest of short lists of *must*-develop skills. As you join me in reviewing self-awareness, my request is to go deep enough in your reflection to identify your opportunities and not so deep that your "lackings" become debilitating. Ironically, I'm asking you, as the reader, to self-assess your own self-awareness! Even for those who've received feedback from others that we are high on the self-awareness scale, there's likely an opportunity to be even more aware. On the other side of this coin, if awareness of your flaws and strengths is a blind spot for you, there are methods to the madness for an entrepreneur to gain a better understanding of themselves. These tools are vast, one of my favorites being the 360-degree feedback system offered through several vendors. Before you rush out to leverage the tool, let's spend some time together exploring this foundational item to build our Purpose Principle.

SELF-AWARENESS

The most significant difference between good and great leaders is their level of self-awareness and their willingness to be better. Self-awareness is built on four pillars. When one has embraced these four pillars in themselves, they begin to fully unlock their potential as leaders. When a leader lacks awareness of who they are, how they impact those around them, and why they do what they do, that leader is tone deaf. The "emperor has no clothes." This lack of awareness creates a wall of self-deception or, worse yet, a coalition of people who tell the leader what they want to hear. I do not mean to be overly dramatic here, but the reality for me with leaders and entrepreneurs who I've seen continue to stall or fail in their efforts mostly centers on the key principle of not being truly honest or even aware of who they really are. Let's get into these four pillars...

PILLAR 1: MINDFULNESS

This is the recognition of the world around you and your place in it. In his book *The 7 Habits of Highly Effective People*, Stephen R. Covey discusses the difference between humans and other animals. We have the ability to remove ourselves from the current state of being, where you can quite literally "take" your mind and observe from the corner of whatever room or place you may be as you read or listen to this book.

You are mindful of your current physical, emotional, and intellectual state. Mindfulness is a key component of self-awareness, as it compels the conscientious observer to refrain from reacting as an animal might when stimulated. You have the ability to suspend your response and consider the stimulus and consequences of your reaction. Great leaders are not impulsive in their responses but have the mindfulness to consider their options and respond appropriately.

Great leaders are not impulsive in their responses but have the mindfulness to consider their options and respond appropriately.

While this is an ability, for some, it may not be part of their natural disposition. You may have to train yourself to be more conscientious and mindful. As you recognize the power of mindfulness, you begin to gain greater control over the world and its never-ending stimuli.

PILLAR 2: ACCOUNTABILITY

One's willingness to own their actions without deflecting responsibility is a building block of true self-awareness. When we become aware of our strengths and weaknesses, the integrity required to be fully accountable compels us to confront the gap between intention and action.

We recognize the need to remove excuses that perpetuate our blind spots and can damage any progress in self-awareness. When we are accountable, we seek feedback: We look for the things that will make us better. Extreme ownership in accountability includes actions that are behavioral, emotional, and performance-driven. Accountability is about internalizing our personal outcomes as well as those of the business.

The greatest leaders do not ask their teams to do what they've not already done or are unwilling to do themselves.

The opposite of accountability is shallowness: It finds fault in others and looks to place blame rather than take responsibility. Accountability is not just holding yourself responsible; it is leading from the front. The greatest leaders do not ask their teams to do what they've not already done or are unwilling to do themselves. The mark of an accountable leader is one who leads from the front.

PILLAR 3: FORGIVENESS

The reality of someone with a high sense of self-awareness can be crippling. To fully recognize one's own faults, weaknesses, mistakes, and disappointments with purity could create an overpowering sense of doubt, frustration, and negativity. It is said that more than 80% of the thoughts an adult has on any given day are negative. Think of that: If the average day is filled with more than 50,000 individual thoughts, and more than 40,000 of them are negative, this can be paralyzing without the concept of forgiveness.

The ability to forgive oneself for the results and consequences of poor decisions or behavior is what allows someone to pick up and try again. It is common to spend time reliving a bad moment, going back and forth between the thoughts and emotions of shame, fear, anger, disappointment, and the awfulization that comes with this human condition. Our minds are powerful, our imaginations endless, and when used as weapons, they can take us to very dark places and keep us there for far too long.

Forgiveness and emotional competency go hand in hand. In my experience, the greatest entrepreneurs have a strong combination of confidence and self-forgiveness. That ability to not "cry over spilled milk" and instead be solution-oriented and growth-inclined is another superpower that can lead to tremendous results.

Just as important as self-forgiveness is the ability to forgive others. I have seen entrepreneurs and founders struggle due to their inability to forgive the follies and mistakes of members of their team. Too often, leaders are unwilling to forgive or let go of things that were, in reality, the same mistakes they themselves made early on in their journeys. Additionally, I've seen owners become so obsessed with perfection that they couldn't settle for progress. The nitpicking and dominating control crushed the people around them, leading to poor company culture and high turnover rates.

The greatest leaders guide the ship with care and control, balancing forgiveness and accountability.

The truth is, until you've developed an enterprise model, the business is you. And your weaknesses as a leader are magnified in a small business. For your business to grow, it is imperative that you strengthen your ability to forgive. This does not mean the business should go without policy, procedure, and performance management. These are necessities for order and discipline. Disciplined people and leadership, as Jim Collins points out in his book *Good to Great,* are key characteristics of great organizations.

The greatest leaders guide the ship with care and control, balancing forgiveness and accountability. When team members are forgiven for mistakes and minor errors, they are more willing to try new things, to be vulnerable, and to be loyal to a leader and an environment that allows for learning and growth.

PILLAR 4: CONFIDENCE

The final pillar of self-awareness, fittingly, goes hand in hand with forgiveness: confidence.

Confidence comes in many forms, but I am not talking about its counterfeits. Confidence is not boastful, it is not haughty, and it is not loud and flashy. Confidence is not conceited or self-absorbed. These forgeries are often projected in popular culture as the essence of someone who is self-assured. In my experience, quite the opposite is true. More often than not, when a leader demonstrates these behaviors, they are masking a deep insecurity that has plagued them for years. These poor imitations are the masks worn by those who lack true confidence.

Real confidence is built from a recipe of key ingredients: optimism, authenticity, competence, resilience, self-efficacy, and self-esteem.

- **Optimism:** A forward-looking mindset that assumes challenges can be overcome. Optimism encourages persistence, which in turn reinforces confidence.
- **Authenticity:** Acting in alignment with one's values and identity. Confidence is strongest when it comes from being genuine rather than trying to impress others.
- **Competence:** Actual skill and knowledge. There is no "fake it till you make it" here. You've been there, done that. Earlier, I referenced the highest level of competence: When one is unconsciously competent, they have mastered the task, and it no longer requires conscious effort. True confidence is grounded in competence; without it, confidence can devolve into overconfidence.
- **Resilience:** The ability to recover from setbacks. This is where forgiveness comes into play. Confidence is reinforced when one learns that failure is temporary and growth is possible.
- **Self-Efficacy:** The belief in one's ability to perform specific tasks or overcome challenges (Bandura, 1977). It comes from practice, preparation, and prior successes.
- **Self-Esteem:** A general sense of self-worth and value. Broader than self-efficacy, it reflects how much one respects and accepts oneself.

Self-acceptance and appreciation for who you are and who you are not bring self-confidence. Your deeper self-awareness also leads to a deeper appreciation for what others bring to the table. It has been said that comparison is the thief of joy. Those who lack confidence struggle to accept themselves for who they are; they are jealous of what others have become or what others have, and that is a very difficult space to live in year after year.

Your deeper self-awareness also leads to a deeper appreciation for what others bring to the table.

To achieve true self-awareness, being comfortable in your own skin and grateful for what you have goes a long way toward good mental health. I am not a psychiatrist and have no formal training in psychology, but I can recognize when the person in front of me has a strong grip on these four pillars. Together, they lead to a core characteristic that drives entrepreneurial success: self-awareness.

Armed with the four pillars of self-awareness, effective leaders take that awareness and are able to recognize and assess in others the emotional competence quotient, or EQ; the intelligence quotient, or IQ; and two forms of CQ, meaning their cultural quotient and their curiosity quotient. Let's explore each a bit further with examples to illustrate, beginning with EQ, or emotional competency, otherwise referred to as emotional intelligence.

Emotional intelligence (EQ) refers to the ability to perceive, understand, manage, and regulate emotions, both one's own and those of others (Goleman, 1995). The value for you as a leader is that when you or a member of your team demonstrates EQ, it enables empathy, active listening, and constructive conflict resolution. Emotional intelligence builds trust and strong interpersonal relationships. When you have it, it helps you motivate others by aligning communication with emotional needs.

A practical example of EQ in action: When you, as a leader with high EQ, notice tension in a team meeting and pause to address concerns before moving forward, preventing disengagement, that's a demonstration of good EQ.

Intelligence quotient (IQ) is the measure of cognitive ability, including logical reasoning, problem-solving, critical thinking, and the capacity to learn. When you or a member of your team demonstrates strong IQ, it provides analytical rigor for strategic decision-making. IQ helps leaders evaluate data, weigh risks, and implement effective solutions. It supports the ability to synthesize complex information into actionable insights.

The reality of IQ is that you may have the greatest human being on the planet working for you, but if they don't have the capacity to learn or think critically in their assigned role, you simply have the wrong person in the right seat. Your ability to secure talent with a high IQ is your ability to grow your business. Without it, limitations can feel like an anchor securing you to a sandbar, leaving you unable to get out to sea.

A practical example of IQ in action is when you, as a leader, can quickly analyze financial data and translate it into practical business decisions. If you don't have it, find someone who does.

Cultural quotient (CQ1) is the ability to understand, adapt to, and work effectively across different cultural contexts. It enhances inclusivity and respect in diverse teams and strengthens collaboration across multicultural settings. Strong cultural intelligence reduces misunderstandings and fosters innovation through diverse perspectives.

A practical example of cultural intelligence in action: when a culturally intelligent leader adapts their communication style while working with partners from different backgrounds, ensuring messages are both respectful and effective.

Curiosity quotient (CQ2) reflects one's drive to learn, explore, and adapt through questioning and discovery. Curiosity encourages innovation by fostering a culture of learning and experimentation. It helps leaders stay adaptable in fast-changing environments. When you have a culture that embraces and fosters curiosity, others are inspired to adopt growth mindsets and pursue continuous improvement.

A practical example of curiosity in action: when a curious leader asks insightful questions during strategic planning, they are challenging assumptions and unlocking new growth opportunities.

As I've outlined these four intelligence quotients, I hope you've concluded that, if your hiring process doesn't currently seek to discover these intelligences in new candidates, it certainly should. Additionally, it would be a great exercise to look at your top performers on the team (and even do some personal introspection) to see if you can identify these Qs as part of the greatness within.

I observe that most entrepreneurs are great at identifying what is missing. They can see it and feel it. They have almost a sixth sense. Even if they don't have a word to describe it, they know something is wrong. And that is an important intuition to have, don't get me wrong. Don't lose that. However, where I see a gap for most people is in failing to define what *makes* greatness. Celebrating these characteristics and explicitly calling them out can deepen a business's success by bringing these elements to the forefront.

When you have a keen awareness of yourself, you're better equipped to recognize the people around you and the unique traits they bring to the table. The best leaders surround themselves with those who complement their blind spots: individuals who are strong in areas where they may not be gifted or competent. Great leaders are willing to set aside their egos and embrace the greatness of others. When you uncover someone's natural genius or unconscious competence, the entrepreneur becomes unstoppable.

The best leaders surround themselves with those who complement their own blind spots.

Personally, I understand the world more clearly when it's organized into a formula or framework. This structure helps me see, interpret, and synthesize the opportunities in front of me and take practical steps to fully capitalize on them. Decades ago, I learned a formula that still resonates with me and with the teams I coach to most effectively manage myself, my business, and the world around me. That formula is:

BAFTA = D

Very simply, it is a progressive set of attributes that build on one another, leading to one's ultimate point of arrival, in this case, one's destiny. The letters in BAFTA = D stand for:

Beliefs, Attitudes, Feelings, Thoughts, Actions = Destiny

Where do each of these come from? How are they defined?

Let's start with attitude.

Attitude is internal, but it is also what you portray to the world around you. The world responds in kind, and you create your own echo chamber, pushing outward and inward simultaneously. You cannot help but react to this with a set of feelings that dictate your thoughts and lead to actions.

Actions are not agnostic. They are not neutral. They tip you one way or another, and their culmination is your destiny.

My hope is that you're able to take this formula and incorporate it into your own life and the lives of those you lead. When you have to have a tough conversation with yourself or someone else, the formula can help you identify where things may be going wrong. If you work backward through the formula, you can uncover the attribute or characteristic that is the root cause of the problem.

Henry David Thoreau once said, *"For every thousand hacking at the leaves of evil, there is one striking at the root."* We deal too much with symptoms. These treatments mask the root cause of the ailment or issue, and we get frustrated when the problem doesn't get solved.

The best entrepreneurs I know seek to focus on the root cause of the problem. They see the issue and look deeper to diagnose: Where is the root cause of these symptoms, and how do we solve it?

With the 5 Principles in this book, you will be exploring the root cause of challenges you may be facing. As we've been exploring the first principle, the precept, my hope is that you are looking in the mirror, assessing who you are, and understanding how your awareness impacts the trajectory of your business. As you go, so goes your business. Unlocking the building blocks of self-awareness and diagnosing where you are and where you need to be is the first step in building the business you've always dreamed of.

Perhaps you've already built something beyond your wildest initial expectations. I'm asking you to consider reinventing yourself and your business to create a 2.0 version of yourself. It's not good enough to have merely arrived at this point. You have more in you to give and more abilities to master.

This journey of life is about who you can become, not who you are. Don't be content; seek greatness. If you've achieved greatness, seek immortality. What is your legacy? What will be said about you when you're gone?

Many of the entrepreneurs we coach go through a "eulogy" exercise. The way this exercise comes together requires the writer to authentically and vulnerably consider the impact they intend to have in each of four groups in life—family, community, professionals, and friends. There is so much more to explore and explain; suffice it to say, it's a great process to go through. The eulogy exercise is linked at the end of this chapter. Follow the QR code and begin with the ultimate end in mind: how you will be remembered, what legacy you've left, and what principles you've instilled in others. I think you'll really appreciate having done it!

We will talk more about accuracy and speed during our Profit Principle, but I think it's a good subject to introduce a leadership evaluation tool here.

In dealing with human beings, fast is slow and slow is fast. Additionally, the outcomes we seek from behavior change are contingent on the choices a leader makes in their interactions with the team members they wish to influence. Too often, unfortunately, our interactions are transactional in nature:

"How are you?"

"Good."

"Sure is cooling down now, isn't it? How's the family?"

"Good, thanks for asking."

Our days are filled with the meaningless transactions of courtesy and acknowledgment, all done with little intention or attention. This, my friend, is speed: the quiet killer of relationships but the fodder of civility (or so we think). Speed treats the current moment as cheap and unimportant. Speed seeks to get this moment out of the way and is focused only on the next. It cares little for the real truth of the interaction and instead looks for a cheap imitation of cordiality.

Now, don't get me wrong: If we treated every interaction as if it were our final one, the intensity and length of each conversation might be overbearing or even inappropriate. It might feel like a mockery of the person or the situation.

Accuracy, on the other hand, treats the moment with its proper weight. It focuses on being effective in the moment, and the exchange between two people leaves both of them edified and better for it. Accuracy gives things, people, and places their proper due. It is not concerned with simply getting through: it deepens connections.

Speed is the status quo and, over time, can cause a relationship to deteriorate.

I recommend you take inventory of your personal and professional life: Where are you sacrificing accuracy for speed? Are you in the moment with the person in front of you, or are you moving from one set of pleasantries to the next without ever really connecting?

Entrepreneurship is a calling, but too many of us fall prey to the grind of the business and its constant needs. We don't truly identify what's valuable and worth our time. We are caught in the whirlwind, and the whirlwind controls us, rather than the other way around.

Accuracy and speed of interactions are powerful indicators of your engagement with the people you love and care for. In this context, self-leadership is the remedy. Reflecting on your ideal and real self and how you move through your day raises an important question: Can you be present and in the moment at all times? Perhaps not. But if you can achieve this presence 80% of the time or more, I suspect you're doing better than most and will reap significant benefits from making that conscious effort.

Leadership matters. This simple statement is as profound as it is true.

Over the course of one's leadership journey—mine now spans more than thirty years—every leader inevitably fails forward, learning how to tap into and unlock their full leadership potential. When personal genius and purpose are fully realized, that's when the sweet spot is found.

The reality is that, as leaders, we are constantly balancing our perceived impact on those we serve across two dimensions: positional power and relational influence. The ideal state is to be perceived as high in both by those we lead.

High positional power means you've demonstrated competence and are seen as a good fit for the role you hold. Your position is respected and seen as influential for the individual you lead and/or the enterprise's business direction. Your role as a leader is significant in the individual's mind, and they see the function as impacting theirs and the business as a whole. High relational influence means you've developed an authentic connection, demonstrated care, and built trust. Another way to say it is that you have made more deposits into the emotional bank account than withdrawals; you know the individual and the world they live in—their likes/dislikes, habits and hobbies, and people that are important to them beyond the walls of the work environment. The real challenge lies in striking this balance effectively with each individual under your leadership.

I refer to this model of understanding as the "Leadership TRIP." Each person you lead perceives you as falling into one of four categories: someone they Tolerate, Respect (both positionally and relationally), feel Indifferent toward, or even Pity.

By reviewing the diagram below, I am aiming to help you identify which quadrant you currently occupy with each individual you lead, how that perception affects your ability to influence them, and, most importantly, how to move from a less-than-ideal quadrant into the respected one.

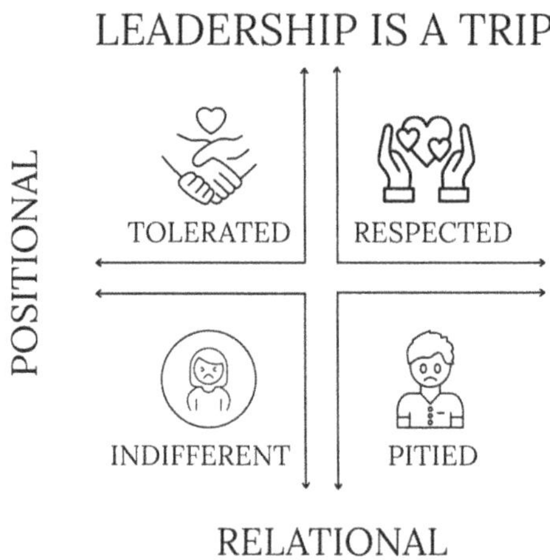

Figure 1. The Leadership TRIP Matrix

THE IMPACTS OF THE LEADERSHIP QUADRANTS

Perhaps it goes without saying that respected leaders achieve better results and outcomes than those in the other quadrants. It is worth noting the differences, so let's start with the obvious: What does a respected leader do, and how does it impact those being led and the organization as a whole?

RESPECTED LEADERS: AUTHORITY WITH AUTHENTIC CONNECTION

Positive Impacts:

- **Enhanced Employee Engagement:** Leaders who are respected cultivate genuine relationships and clear positional authority (this is how the team sees your position or title and its relevance to the individual's daily or future growth and your position's significance to the business itself), driving deeper commitment, higher job satisfaction, and elevated discretionary effort among team members (Gallup, 2021).
- **Increased Organizational Effectiveness:** Respected leaders foster trust, clarity, and accountability, enhancing overall performance, operational efficiency, and strategic alignment (Northouse, 2021).
- **Higher Retention and Talent Attraction:** Teams led by respected leaders experience lower turnover and attract higher-quality talent due to a positive organizational reputation and appealing culture (Kouzes & Posner, 2017).
- **Innovation and Adaptability:** Respected leaders encourage open dialogue, trust, and psychological safety, fostering an environment conducive to innovation, adaptability, and continuous improvement (Edmondson, 2019).
- **Strong Organizational Culture:** By demonstrating integrity, consistency, and care, respected leaders build and sustain strong organizational cultures that significantly contribute to long-term competitive advantage and organizational resilience (Sinek, 2014).

Leadership perception significantly influences team performance, organizational culture, and overall effectiveness. Leaders perceived in the pitied, tolerated, or indifferent quadrants experience substantial negative impacts, hindering both relationships and organizational outcomes.

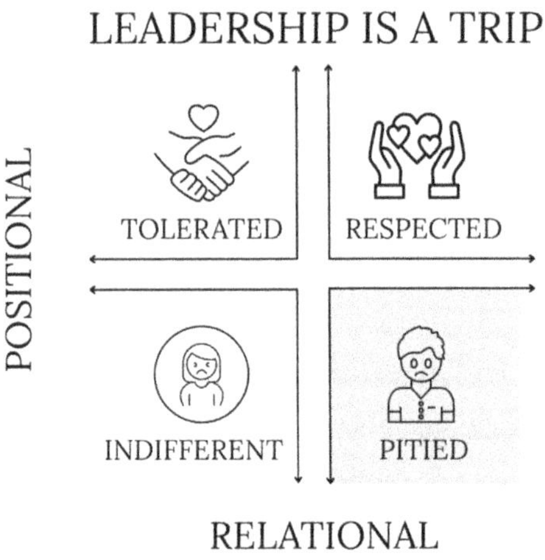

Figure 2. Pitied Leaders: Empathy without Respect

Detrimental Impacts:

- **Reduced Organizational Effectiveness:** Leaders who are pitied (but liked) lack authority and credibility. Their decisions are frequently questioned or disregarded, leading to inefficiencies and slow organizational progress (Goleman, Boyatzis, & McKee, 2013).
- **Lowered Team Morale:** While teams may feel empathy toward a pitied leader, they often lose motivation, experiencing frustration due to perceived ineffectiveness. This, in turn, dampens team morale and productivity (Lencioni, 2002).

- **Limited Professional Growth:** Pitied leaders are often excluded from critical strategic conversations or decisions, limiting their personal and professional development and diminishing their career trajectory.

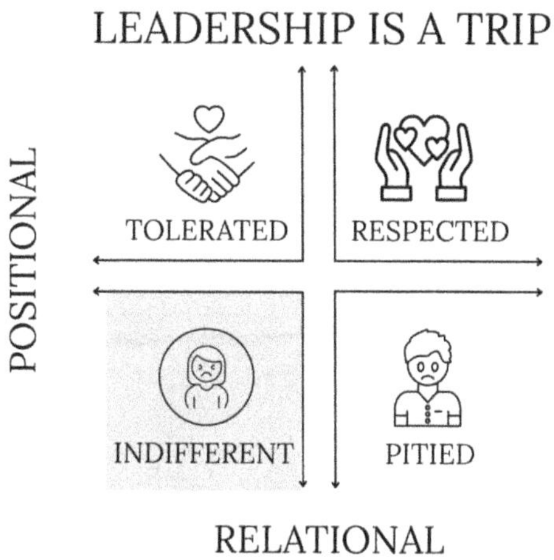

Figure 3. Indifferent Leaders: Disengagement and Disconnection

Detrimental Impacts:

- **Stagnation and Lack of Innovation:** Indifference breeds disengagement. Teams led by leaders for whom they are indifferent lack direction and motivation, resulting in stagnant work environments with limited creativity and innovation (Kouzes & Posner, 2017).
- **Reduced Accountability:** Without relational or positional influence, leaders for whom their direct reports are indifferent fail to foster a culture of accountability. Team performance suffers as the organization experiences an environment of unclear expectations, and a sense of ambiguous responsibilities becomes the norm (Covey, 2004).

- **Poor Organizational Culture:** Leaders toward whom their team is indifferent see an erosion of trust, collaboration, and organizational loyalty, eventually resulting in a fragmented and unproductive organizational culture (Sinek, 2014).

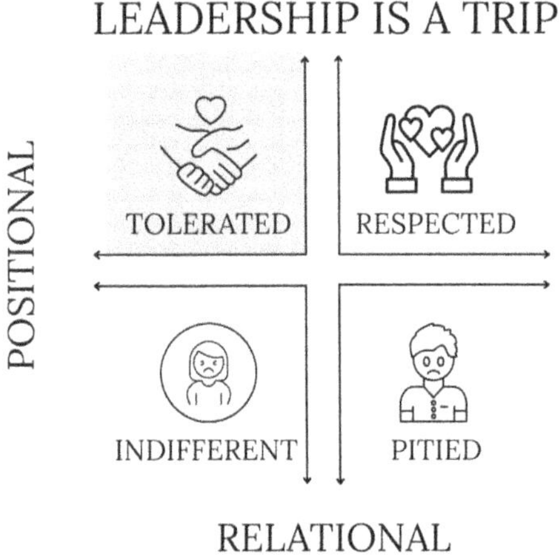

Figure 4. Tolerated Leaders: Authority without Connection

Detrimental Impacts:

- **Minimal Employee Engagement:** Employees under tolerated leaders comply out of a sense of obligation rather than genuine commitment. This compliance without engagement limits innovation, creativity, and discretionary effort, which are critical for organizational success (Gallup, 2021).
- **High Employee Turnover:** Without meaningful relational connections, employees may seek workplaces with more supportive leadership environments, leading to higher turnover rates and increased organizational costs (Northouse, 2021).

- **Resentment and Dysfunction:** The purely positional authority of tolerated leaders often fosters resentment, passive-aggressive behavior, and organizational dysfunction, significantly impairing team dynamics and collaborative efforts (Maxwell, 2018).

WHY THESE DOWNSIDE IMPACTS MATTER

Each leadership quadrant outside of "Respected" limits organizational growth, damages employee engagement, and weakens organizational culture. Organizations with leaders stuck in these less-than-ideal quadrants face higher costs related to turnover, reduced efficiency, lower innovation capacity, and compromised competitive advantage.

Moving toward respected leadership, which balances positional power with relational influence, provides teams with clarity, motivation, and engagement, significantly improving organizational effectiveness and health.

WHAT CAN BE DONE

If you find yourself in one of the PIT quadrants (Pitied, Indifferent, or Tolerated), what can you do? On the following page are the starting points and the leadership tactics you need to implement to migrate from the "PIT" to the Respected quadrant.

Pathway 1: Pitied → Tolerated → Respected

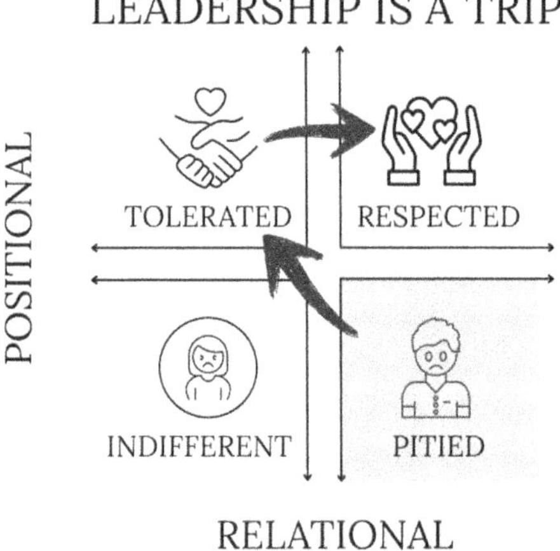

Starting Point (Pitied):

- Low positional power, high relational empathy (people like you personally but doubt your leadership effectiveness).

Step 1: Pitied → Tolerated

- **Demonstrate Competence:** Clearly articulate vision and responsibilities; clarify and enforce accountability.
- **Follow Through on Commitments:** Ensure reliability by delivering on promises consistently, building positional credibility.
- **Increase Decisiveness:** Make clear, timely, and necessary leadership decisions.

Step 2: Tolerated → Respected

- **Strengthen Relationships with Authenticity:** Actively listen, respond genuinely, and regularly engage team members in meaningful conversations.
- **Recognize Contributions:** Celebrate individual and team achievements publicly.
- **Model Organizational Values:** Exemplify behaviors reflecting the core values and expectations of the organization.

Pathway 2: Indifferent → Tolerated → Respected

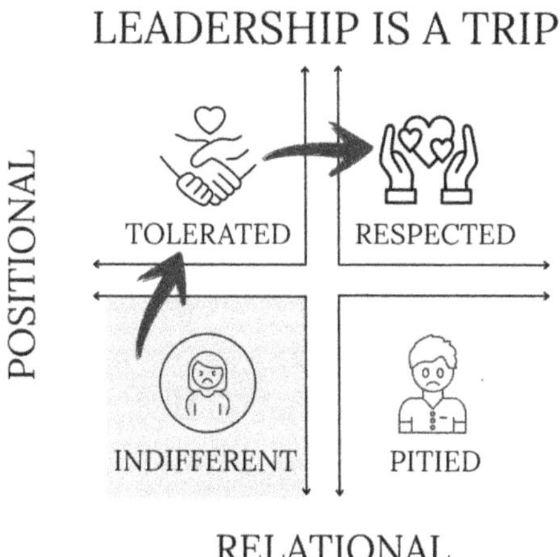

Starting Point (Indifferent):

- Low relational and low positional influence (the team neither connects personally nor respects your position).

Step 1: Indifferent → Tolerated

- **Increase Visibility and Engagement:** Participate consistently and openly in team activities and decision-making processes.
- **Set and Communicate Clear Expectations:** Provide structure, clarity, and accountability, establishing positional authority.
- **Regular and Structured Feedback:** Offer constructive feedback routinely, showing you're involved and committed.

Step 2: Tolerated → Respected

- **Invest in Personal Connections:** Hold regular one-on-one interactions, demonstrating genuine interest in team members' professional growth and personal well-being.
- **Empower Your Team:** Trust them with meaningful projects and decision-making autonomy.
- **Consistent Recognition:** Acknowledge and reward behaviors aligned with organizational culture and goals.

Pathway 3: Indifferent → Pitied → Tolerated → Respected

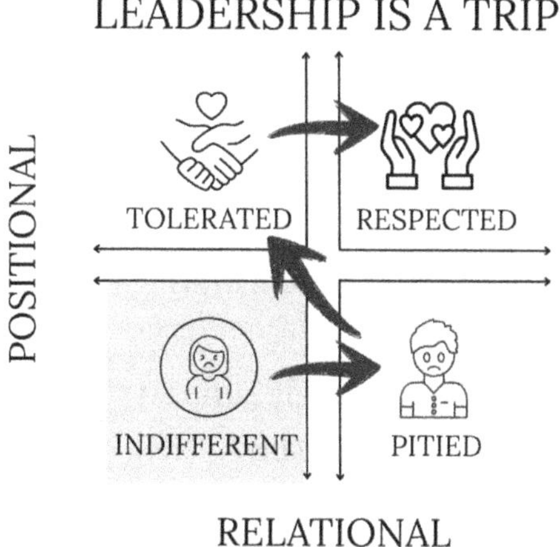

(This indirect path acknowledges the possibility of first increasing relational empathy before positional strength.)

Step 1: Indifferent → Pitied

- **Humanize Leadership:** Share your own challenges and stories openly, building initial relational connections through vulnerability.
- **Personal Outreach:** Invest time individually to better understand team members' personal circumstances and concerns.

Step 2: Pitied → Tolerated

- **Address Competence Concerns:** Clearly define roles and expectations; demonstrate effectiveness through actions.

- **Hold Yourself Accountable:** Show disciplined follow-through, decisiveness, and improved professional effectiveness.

Step 3: Tolerated → Respected

- **Deepen Trust:** Proactively solicit and implement team feedback, consistently demonstrating respect for employees' input.
- **Mentor and Coach:** Actively support the professional growth of team members, showcasing genuine care and investment.

<u>Pathway 4: Tolerated → Respected</u>

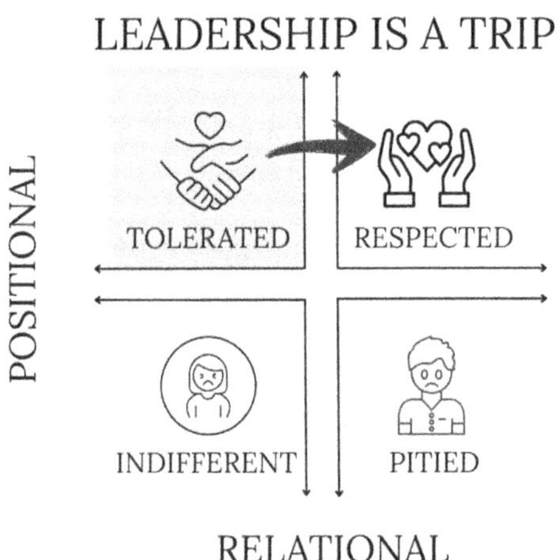

Starting Point (Tolerated):

- Adequate positional influence, low relational strength (team complies primarily out of duty or obligation).

Direct Step: Tolerated → Respected

- **Authentic Relationship Building:** Actively seek feedback, listen empathetically, and demonstrate genuine care in response.
- **Lead by Example:** Demonstrate integrity, consistency, and transparency to build relational respect.
- **Proactive Recognition:** Regularly and sincerely appreciate team members' unique contributions, reinforcing positive, relational connections.

Pathway 5: Pitied → Indifferent → Tolerated → Respected

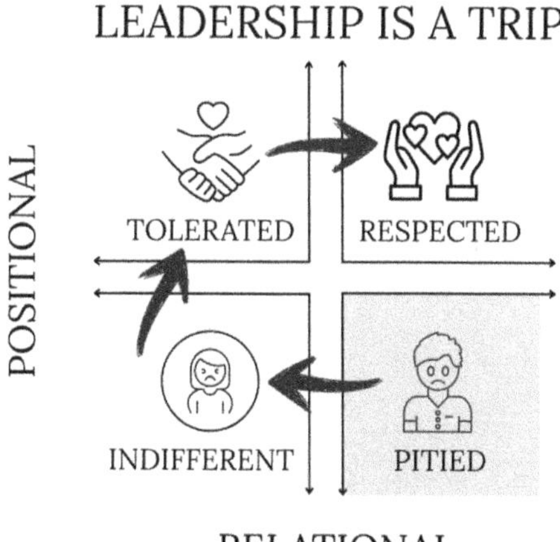

(This less common path involves losing relational influence initially before regaining it along with positional power.)

Step 1: Pitied → Indifferent

- **Reduce Over-Personalization:** Begin to distance overly personal interactions that might undermine perceptions of professionalism. Adopt a more neutral approach to reset relational boundaries.

Step 2: Indifferent → Tolerated

- **Re-establish Positional Clarity:** Define clear expectations and enforce structured accountability, showcasing reliability and decisiveness to restore confidence in leadership capability.

Step 3: Tolerated → Respected

- **Rebuild Authentic Connections:** Gradually reintroduce relational warmth, balanced with clear professional boundaries and authentic care for employees' welfare and development.
- **Consistent Leadership Presence:** Maintain transparency and active engagement in daily leadership interactions.

Summary of All Possible Paths to "Respected": Path Sequence of Quadrants

- Pathway 1 (common): Pitied → Tolerated → Respected
- Pathway 2 (common): Indifferent → Tolerated → Respected
- Pathway 3 (alternative): Indifferent → Pitied → Tolerated → Respected
- Pathway 4 (direct): Tolerated → Respected
- Pathway 5 (less common): Pitied → Indifferent → Tolerated → Respected

As you reflect on your relationship with those you're responsible for leading, I'd ask you to give some thought to the currency of trust and culture.

In the evolving landscape of modern business, trust and culture represent two of the most critical yet intangible assets. While strategy may offer direction, structure, and measurable objectives, it is trust and culture that determine whether strategies are embraced, sustained, and executed effectively.

Trust can be measured, nurtured, and exchanged like currency, and culture serves as the invisible architecture shaping every decision, interaction, and outcome.

Earlier, I quoted the renowned Peter Drucker as saying, "*Execution* eats strategy for breakfast." He is also known for a modification to that statement that is equally apropos when it comes to the ecosystem you've created in your business. He observed, "*Culture* eats strategy for breakfast." This assertion underscores the primacy of culture in organizational life and its deep interdependence with trust.

While culture or trust may not be truly formulaic, there is value in quantifying how your business is enabling trust in the ecosystem you've designed. Building on organizational practices like credibility, reliability, intimacy, and orientation, my argument is that businesses that prioritize trust and cultivate culture outperform those that merely rely on strategic intent.

Ultimately, there's an anatomy to trust: It is the combination of character and competence.

Trust is often perceived as intangible, yet it can be broken into definable components. A widely referenced equation frames trust as a balance of credibility, reliability, intimacy, and self-orientation:

Trust = (Credibility + Reliability + Intimacy) ÷ Self-Orientation

- Credibility reflects the confidence others have in one's words and expertise.
- Reliability is the demonstrated consistency between promises and delivery.
- Intimacy captures the safety and emotional closeness one fosters to enable openness and collaboration.
- Self-orientation refers to whether motives are inwardly focused (selfish) or outwardly directed (altruistic).

This formula reveals a paradox: Trust grows not from perfection, but from consistent alignment of character and competency. Character ensures motives are aligned with the greater good, while competence ensures the ability to deliver on promises.

In this sense:

Trust = Character + Competence

And when self-orientation is high, trust erodes, regardless of skill or credibility.

The better entrepreneur recognizes this self-orientation, first in themselves, and then in the people they've surrounded themselves with. Culture can flourish or erode one person at a time as you fine-tune the self-orientation makeup.

Self-orientation acts as the magnetic force in the compass, leading a person closer to, or further from, the trust of others.

As I stated earlier, for the small business, "As goes the founder, so goes the business." The founder's values, communication style, and decision-making create a cultural imprint that cascades throughout the organization. A founder who models outward orientation, transparency, and reliability lays the groundwork for enduring trust. Conversely, a founder whose motives are inwardly focused often creates cultures of suspicion and fragility.

A founder who models outward orientation, transparency, and reliability lays the groundwork for enduring trust.

If you see culture suffering, start with the mirror before running toward the window.

Consider the goals you've set for your team. Are they perceived as benefiting only the owner, or do they connect the entire team to incentives tied to purpose, passion, or a shared cause?

Beyond formulas, trust functions as a currency that is exchanged daily within organizations. Just as money facilitates economic activity, trust facilitates relational and organizational activity. Every agreement, delegation, and handshake is an exchange of trust.

Francis Fukuyama's seminal work on social capital frames trust as a cornerstone of both economic and organizational life. I have in mind particularly *Trust: The Social Virtues and the Creation of Prosperity* (1995) and his later reflections in *Problems and Perspectives in Management* (2022).

Societies and businesses with high levels of generalized trust can transact with less friction, fewer formalities, and reduced regulatory burdens. In contrast, where trust is lacking, organizations must rely on elaborate systems of oversight, contracts, and monitoring.

If you tend to micromanage, your team will inevitably require more rules, audits, and oversight to function. Much like the Pygmalion effect, employees tend to become what you expect them to be.

I remember being fascinated in college during an organizational behavior course when we studied McGregor's Theory X and Theory Y:

- Theory X assumes employees are inherently lazy and must be coerced and controlled, leading to an authoritarian style.
- Theory Y assumes employees are self-motivated and seek responsibility, leading to a participative and democratic style.

The better entrepreneurs I have seen might have marginal influence from the X and the Y, undoubtedly, but have the flexibility within themselves to realize that Pygmalion's Effect is a fundamental truth in human nature. In many cases, we become what we're expected to become, or rather, we are who we allow our conditions and nurture to influence us to be. This whole concept is utterly fascinating to me and inspires me to recall a potentially cryptic chapter in the Tao Te Ching:

The wise have no fixed opinion.
They take the people's opinion as their own.
Those who are good, I treat as good.
Those who are bad, I treat as good.
That's the perfection of goodness.
Those who are honest, I treat as honest.
Those who are dishonest, I treat as honest.
That's the perfection of honesty.
Among the people, the wise reserve their opinion
And live in harmony with them.
The expectations you set as a business owner largely determine how your people respond and perform.

To be clear, I'm not suggesting that trust and formal systems are in opposition. Rather, they are mutually reinforcing when balanced correctly. Rules, systems, and regulations create clarity and reduce ambiguity, but they must be grounded in trust. Otherwise, they become bureaucratic "taxes" on growth. The flexible leader realizes the balance and beauty of a culture that is nurtured by simple and clear beliefs that bring the participant to self-governance.

In a vacuum of trust, systems multiply and ultimately hinder agility.

That's why businesses should treat trust as both a relational asset and a performance multiplier, investing in it as deliberately as they would in capital or infrastructure.

The most effective leaders I've worked with, especially in small businesses, are maniacally focused on culture. Their purposeful attention to culture and the systems that support it separates good companies from great ones.

Let's explore the relationship between trust and culture. While trust provides the currency of relationships, culture provides the context in which that currency circulates.

Culture, though difficult to define, is always felt. It's the lived experience of shared values, norms, and meaning. As Drucker emphasized, culture dominates strategy because culture determines whether a strategy is embraced or resisted.

But how do you facilitate culture? It happens through storytelling.

Culture is not transmitted through policy manuals alone. It lives in the stories people tell. Every organization holds narratives that reinforce its values:

- Stories of how a leader supported a client.
- Stories of a team overcoming a setback.
- Stories of integrity upheld in a difficult moment.

The presence or absence of such stories determines whether values are aspirational words or lived realities.

THE STUMP SPEECH: A LEADER'S TOOL

The Entrepreneurial Operating System (EOS) shares a powerful storytelling tool: the stump speech.

In the nineteenth century, traveling politicians would often find a raised spot, like a tree stump, to deliver their messages. Thus, the "stump speech" was born.

For today's entrepreneur, the stump speech should be crafted intentionally. I've seen too many leaders fail to inspire simply because they weren't prepared. A strong stump speech should include your company's core values, supported by real, specific stories of team members embodying those values. The more personal and recognizable the examples, the more meaningful the message.

Prepare five to seven values, each with two to three supporting stories. This gives you a repertoire of ten to twenty ready-made stories that illustrate your values in action. Don't shy away from sharing stories that reflect the antithesis of those values, too, focusing on what happens when they're ignored or betrayed.

I've seen too many leaders fail to inspire simply because they weren't prepared.

The point here is that to drive your culture forward, you must become a great storyteller.

Culture cannot be left to chance; it must be nurtured constantly through values, principles, or a credo. Leaders must not only articulate values but also embody them.

For example, a company that claims "clients first" must tell and retell stories of client advocacy, and leaders must model behaviors that put clients above personal or political gain. As Emerson once said, "Your actions speak so loudly, I cannot hear what you are saying."

This is why your selection of values is so critical. If you or your team don't have the passion, interest, or ability to live up to them, don't pick them.

This brings us back to our alignment model: "ideal self" vs. "real self." Culture is built or lost in the behaviors, habits, and systems of accountability you create in between. It also aligns with the trust equation:

- High credibility and reliability foster cultures of excellence.
- Intimacy creates cultures of belonging.
- Outward orientation builds cultures of service.

Together, these elements produce an ecosystem where employees, clients, and partners trust both the intent and capability of the organization.

For small businesses, trust and culture are magnified because they are inseparable from the founder. Entrepreneurs who treat trust as a currency and culture as their first "product" often find themselves with loyal employees and customers long before strategies or structures are perfected.

I've had business owners tell me that the team comes before the customer. You might hear that and think it's heresy, and maybe you're right. But the best cultures I've seen are those where leaders intentionally invest in individual employees to ensure they adhere to, believe in, and outwardly demonstrate company values.

Consider two paths:

1. A founder builds systems to control behavior because they mistrust employees. The culture becomes one of compliance and minimal initiative. As the founder goes, so goes the business. I've worked with some incredibly strong personalities along the way. In my observation, those business owners who have not developed their leadership abilities and acumen are stifling growth. Typically, this distrustful environment is the leader's fault. They usually look outward and have conditioned themselves to find fault, errors, issues, and problems. It didn't start that way. The founder developed this kind of environment over many years. It is the frog that boils with an ever-so-slight increase of temperature. They built the business through such brute force of will and a unique talent and never spent the time to really develop those around them. This first camp of founders put all of their energy into doing more themselves and left the others they hired to "figure it out," who turned around and said, "I had to figure it out, and anyone worth their salt that will be on my team must do the same." The trust was never extended beyond their own work, and usually, the work product of anyone else is seen as inferior. There is a deeply rooted pride in what they've built and are building, and it destroys scale and the next generation. With every mistake made and fault found, they are further proving their point while pushing their team to feel like nothing is ever good enough and say, "What's the point in trying?" The environment leads to people who just show up, tolerate their boss, and collect a paycheck. This description may feel harsh. I do not mean to offend, but offense is in the eye of the beholder. Someone must tell the truth here, and if the leader is to achieve the mission of the organization, some self-awareness and a look inward can make all the difference. I would think of it this way: If I knew there was one thing I needed to discover and change about myself that would lead to my business being worth three times what it is today, would I change it? For most of us, we do not change much unless the pain or discomfort is consequential enough to do so. When we are looking to migrate from the real self to the ideal self, the habits, systems, and behaviors that bring us over the chasm are uncomfortable and even painful. If you are reading this and it seems a bit pointed, perhaps there's an opportunity to make a change.

2. The second path is a founder who invests in credibility, reliability, and intimacy while maintaining outward orientation. There is a sharing along the way—humility, in the fact that the founder simply can't do it all themselves—but with a subtle difference from Path 1 above: They seek someone who can do it better than they can and are willing to lay aside their ego to get this done. They take the people with them on the journey. Remember, "if you want to go fast, go alone... If you want to go far, go together." Going together can be frustrating and feel like you're taking a step backward at times. And perhaps you are! The strategy here includes patience, discipline, and a willingness to fail so that there is learning. Human beings grow when they experience success and failure. I'm not talking about a complete system failure. You should never allow someone on the team to have the ability to risk the future of the business. However, controlled environments that allow for mistakes teach the participant more than just the error and the right way to do the task. Even more important is the condition that allows them to be supported and the willingness to invest in their development. Perfection may be the ideal, but it likely does not happen consistently in the real world. To err is human, and when the leader creates an environment that recognizes humanity and those humans feel safe, these are the teams that charge the greatest of hills together and *win*! The result: employees reciprocate with trust, innovation, and discretionary effort.

The difference lies not in strategy but in the currency of trust and the richness of the soil in which culture is nurtured.

Ultimately (and contrary to common belief), trust and culture are not abstract ideals. They are measurable, actionable, and essential. Trust, as defined by credibility, reliability, intimacy, and orientation, provides both a formula and a daily currency of exchange. Culture, though intangible, is the environment where trust thrives, reinforced through values, stories, and leadership.

Fukuyama's research reminds us: In the absence of trust, systems and regulations multiply and become taxes on growth. Drucker reminds us that no matter how sophisticated the strategy, culture determines its success. For leaders and entrepreneurs, the mandate is clear: Build trust as your currency and cultivate culture as your competitive advantage. In doing so, organizations unlock resilience, adaptability, and sustainable prosperity.

Build trust as your currency and cultivate culture as your competitive advantage.

With our Purpose Principle in place, we've done much soul-searching and reflection.

As you go, so goes the business.

Now, let's turn our attention to the People Principle in your organization and how you can help people become their best selves!

PRINCIPLE 2: PEOPLE

A favorite quip of mine is, "This business would be a lot easier if no people were involved." While it may be humorous, it is simply unrealistic in most businesses to expect to function and grow without human capital. For most businesses, payroll and the costs associated with the people on their team are their largest expense and their biggest investment.

The war for top talent is real, and the entrepreneur who captures the best people has the greatest chance of competing and winning against their competitors.

We started this book with the idea that entrepreneurship is lonely; there are millions of us scattered across the globe, but it can feel like you're all alone. The DNA of an entrepreneur is unique. The willingness to sacrifice, take significant risks, and bet on oneself are all characteristics that make us who we are.

Content that I've admired, drawn from over fifty years of research, is documented by The Rewilding Group. They describe members of the team you work with as either builders or protectors. A builder is one who is looking outward, seeking to stretch the business's growth, and is willing to take chances and break a few things along the way. A protector is one who is looking inward. They work to insulate the existing business from threats, whether real or perceived, to the way things are.

I've found this language invaluable in coaching teams on how to think about the characteristics of their members and the fact that both are needed. Builders and protectors sometimes don't get along and may struggle to understand one another. But in the end, your business needs the right ratio of builders to protectors.

For our purposes, an additional classification is worth exploring to further clarify the nature of the entrepreneur and the people surrounding them. In my experience, you have a few players on any team. The categories I've chosen for identification are the entrepreneur, of course, and the intrapreneur.

If you're unable to classify members of your team in one of these two categories, you may have a people issue. Keeping people on the team who are not one of these two types is dangerous. If you have someone who is just there for the "J.O.B.," they are harming your culture.

Too many business owners make the mistake of thinking there are neutral or harmless players on the team. Not so. People are either contributing to or detracting from your productivity, culture, and client/customer experience.

Now, this isn't to say that if someone is underperforming during a season of their career, they should be jettisoned. Everyone has their moments or seasons when they need grace, tough love, training, or a reset. The greatest leaders I've seen recognize the gray area here and give people chances to do and be better.

Leaders take people to places they would not have considered, let alone gone themselves.

Leaders take people to places they would not have considered, let alone gone themselves.

I've personally conducted thousands of interviews and over 100 exit interviews. I've had countless conversations with leadership teams struggling with an employee or partner who was not only worth saving but also had incredible potential beyond their current underperformance. This is the essence of a great comeback story, one that can be part of the storytelling that enhances and strengthens the culture of the firm. Who doesn't love a great comeback? However, there are people on your team who are a cancer to what you're building. They may be quiet, but they are killers. Eye-rollers, gossipers, and naysayers to anything they simply don't want to do. Metaphorically, they are slashing the tires and lighting your business on fire. These people need to be removed.

There are myriad reasons why someone may not be a great fit, and perhaps it's not entirely their fault. But almost without exception, every team I've helped to work through the process of "offloading" this kind of team member finds out that they waited too long. The leadership team starts to hear the real story; the rest of the group had been holding back and dealing with the underperformer quietly and painfully. Many teams I coach make the choice of being understaffed, overcapacity, or stretched a bit thin, rather than having someone like this on the team. In my experience, it is *always* better to be decisive and remove these people sooner rather than later.

Of course, there are situations that require care, such as employees who are litigious, part of a protected class, or appear to have a specialized or complex skill set that makes removal difficult. Don't be reckless, but do be deliberate. You *must* protect the talent on your team, and the best way to do that is to remove the human capital that is impeding their ability to perform.

ENTREPRENEUR OR INTRAPRENEUR

For those members of the team who should be on the team, you'll see on the followin page a side-by-side comparison of the characteristics of the entrepreneur and the intrapreneur. This is likely not an exhaustive list, but it provides a strong sense of the differences.

A little self-diagnosis, along with some reflection by the team member, can be healthy. This helps tremendously when you're in a situation where an employee is interested in ownership. In an upcoming chapter, we'll talk about the three rungs of the ownership ladder and how to create a system that facilitates a place for all members of the team to participate.

You might want to take the list on the following page and a piece of paper, write down the names of the members of your organization, and see if you can identify whether someone has the potential to be an entrepreneur alongside you or if they are and always will be an incredible contributor who simply lacks the qualities of an entrepreneur. By saying this, I do not intend to imply that one is more or less valuable than the other. Nor should anyone feel that they have to change themselves to move from one side to the other. If the *why* of entrepreneurship is strong enough, the right person will go through any *how* to get there.

Changes in behavior are very difficult. There needs to be a conscious and constant effort to go from who you are to who you want to be.

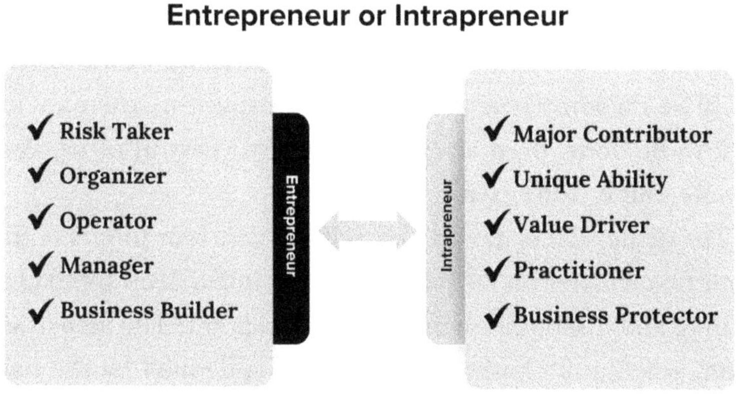

Entrepreneur or Intrapreneur

Entrepreneur

✔ Risk Taker
✔ Organizer
✔ Operator
✔ Manager
✔ Business Builder

Intrapreneur

✔ Major Contributor
✔ Unique Ability
✔ Value Driver
✔ Practitioner
✔ Business Protector

Figure 5: Entrepreneur vs. Intrapreneur

As a corporate sales leader and executive, I've learned through some hard knocks, trial and error, and formal education that past behavior is a strong indicator of future behavior when it comes to human beings. The tiger and the stripes analogy, if you will. This isn't to say that everyone stays the same or that there's no room for people to change. What I am saying is that changes in behavior are very difficult. There needs to be a conscious and constant effort to go from who you are to who you want to be.

THE ALIGNMENT MODEL

I learned the idea of the alignment model from Doug Lennick, who now runs an organization called Think 2 Perform. Along my journey, the alignment model framework has been incredibly valuable to me, first, as I worked to be self-aware in my own state, and second, as I led and mentored others around me.

The idea behind the alignment model is that we all have an ideal picture of who we could and should be. This goes beyond one facet and covers the full gamut of our existence: health, wealth, relationships, communication, love—the list is endless. Unfortunately, every one of us is failing in multiple areas simultaneously as we fall short of who we want to be and who we actually are. If we do some true and honest introspection, there's a lot of work to be done, even among the most successful of us. Perfect mortals simply don't exist.

The actual self is flawed and, without the four pillars outlined in our first chapter on Purpose, could fall into a deep spiral of self-loathing and disappointment. Forgiveness is key! The area of separation, whether a chasm or a thin line, is defined by the habits, rituals, routines, and self-management we put in place. The alignment model is simply a framework to help understand the "how" of becoming your best self.

In the following image, you can see how these three components of the alignment model come together: Our aspirations or ideals can only be bridged by the systems and habits we put in place to take our current self across the gap.

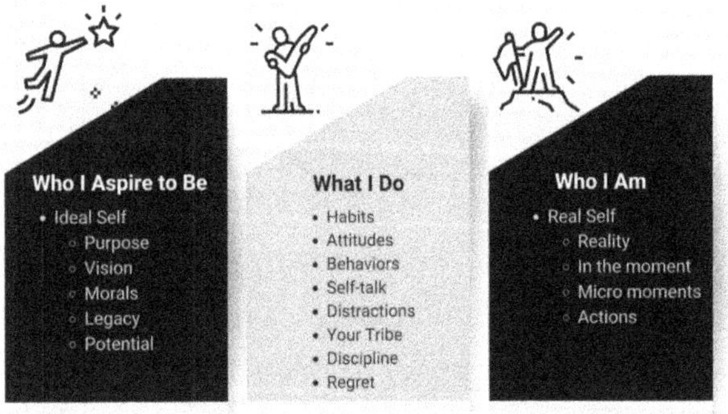

Figure 6: The Alignment Model

The most noble pursuit any individual can have in this life is in the becoming. Ezra Taft Benson, former United States Secretary of Agriculture and religious leader, said it best: "Some of the greatest battles you will face will be fought within the silent chambers of your own soul."

As you contemplate this statement, your mind may wander in many directions. Where I personally linger is on the idea that everyone, without exception, is facing a battle: an internal struggle shaped by a unique combination of faults, follies, addictions, tendencies, and more. These are the stumbling blocks that get in the way of achieving our ideal selves. And the battles won in this silent, unseen space are often the most profound.

Of course, we cheer when we witness incredible feats accomplished by men and women throughout history. But none compare to the wars we've fought and won within ourselves. Why is that? Because those victories are deeply personal and uniquely meaningful. For me, achieving something great within myself is far more valuable than watching someone else's success. Valuable? Absolutely. But the most impactful victories will always be the personal ones.

When you encounter someone who is moldable, humble, and hungry, you've found a gem. That person has the potential to grow into a skilled and highly competent member of your team. The real question is, are you good at developing people? Do you have the energy for it?

If you haven't experienced recent and relevant success in this area, your answer is likely "no." And suppose your core competency isn't developing talent from the ground up, then you have a decision to make. In that case, either find someone who *is* great at it or invest more in hiring people who are already "ready"—those who have the mindset, the skills, and the drive to help you build your business.

But here's the reality: You go to war with the people you have, not the people you wish you had. Developing talent and caring for your people is just as important as developing your business. In truth, your people *are* your business. Your future depends on them. That's why it's imperative to invest in them.

You go to war with the people you have, not the people you wish you had. Developing talent and caring for your people is just as important as developing your business.

Early in my career, I worked as a training manager. Part of my role was onboarding novice individuals and equipping them to become self-sufficient, competent advisers for retail clients. These recruits came from a wide variety of backgrounds and experiences. Sometimes we were right in our hiring decisions, and sometimes we were wrong.

At a training conference with fellow managers, the topic turned to the cost of development: the time, energy, and resources spent for what often felt like minimal return. One trainer posed a common concern:

"What if I spend all this time, energy, and effort training them, and then they leave? I'll have wasted my time and the company's resources."

A respected leader in the room responded with a statement I've never forgotten:

"What if you *don't* train them, and they stay?"

That response has stuck with me. I still share it often when leadership teams feel burned out from the development grind. The message is simple and powerful: If you're going to invest your firm's resources into hiring someone, don't do it halfway. Give them your best effort. They deserve nothing less. If you can't commit to that, you shouldn't have hired them in the first place.

When an entrepreneur and their leadership team are brutally honest with themselves, they come to realize that investing in new hires must be intentional: defined, documented, and delivered with purpose.

Too many business owners face turnover or underperformance simply because they fail to invest appropriately in the people they've brought on board. They treat hiring as an endpoint rather than the beginning of a longer, intentional process.

If you have an incredible intrapreneur in front of you, someone who *wants* to contribute, put them in the best position to succeed. Do that, and you'll likely have a loyal, driven, and high-impact team member for decades to come.

If you're going to invest your firm's resources into hiring someone, don't do it halfway. Give them your best effort.

Another way to describe members of a team, drawn from Fischer's book *Navigating the Growth Curve*, is by categorizing people as either builders or protectors of the business. Just because someone on the team is hesitant to jump headfirst into the entrepreneur's next big idea doesn't mean they're trying to sabotage progress; rather, they're acting as a protector, safeguarding what's already been built: the culture, the processes, and the systems in place.

The protector is a critical part of the team, ensuring the business can sustain the entrepreneur's drive and focus on growth. The builder, on the other hand, is forward-looking, spotting opportunities and "charging the hill." However, builders can sometimes act impulsively, calling out "Charge!" without fully considering the consequences for the team or the broader ecosystem.

The balance between protectors and builders is the homeostasis that your business, viewed as a living organism, requires to thrive. One of the most valuable insights I've taken from Fischer's work is the recognition that the best builder-to-protector ratio changes over time. Too many individuals of either mindset can push or pull the business into dangerous territory. Understanding your people, their mindsets, values, and potential risks, is essential when applying your People Principle.

I'm a strong advocate of the Entrepreneurial Operating System (EOS), based on the concepts in Gino Wickman's book *Traction*. A core part of this system involves defining company values to clearly articulate the intended culture. One key concept is "Right People, Right Seat." This starts by defining your organizational structure, clarifying the essential "seats on the bus" needed to run the business effectively. Once the structure is in place, you can begin filling those seats with individuals who get it, want it, and have the capacity to do it. The people you attract and retain will reflect both you and the systems you've designed for assessing, onboarding, and developing them.

As we'll explore with the next principle, Process, you'll see that without a structured system for developing your people, you can't expect consistent results in human capital. It's crucial to have an assessment process to determine whether someone is the right fit and whether they will continue to be.

If you've clearly articulated your firm's values, these can act as a barometer or litmus test for team alignment. For example, if your organization has six core values, a team member should consistently demonstrate at least four of them to remain on the team. These values serve as your performance standard. If someone falls below that standard, they should be made aware of it, given clear examples, and offered a specific action plan to get back on track, typically within thirty to ninety days.

Allowing underperformance to persist can be a culture killer, especially in living out company values. EOS includes a powerful tool called the People Analyzer, which helps you define your minimum standard. Leadership teams can use it at least annually, or more frequently, to assess alignment and performance.

There's nothing more valuable than a clear system when dealing with complex and subjective matters like people and values. The People Analyzer transforms the intangible into the tangible, offering a practical method for evaluating team members.

There's nothing more valuable than a clear system when dealing with complex and subjective matters like people and values.

Additionally, you should have some form of third-party assessment process that becomes your firm's language to articulate who someone is and how they contribute. Pick one or two that work for your team and go deep, whether you use CliftonStrengths Finder, DiSC, Myers-Briggs, Working Genius, or something else. I've worked with a team that developed their own "baseball cards" that included individuals' assessment results, likes/dislikes, core values, interesting facts, and a few other meaningful items. They used these to introduce new and existing team members to one another. I've seen other teams do the same, even adding a moment in regular, full-team meetings to review and introduce people. These are the kinds of actions that build culture in a significant way. If you're looking for a great tool for core values identification, there's a free one on the Think 2 Perform website, which will make a great addition to your team's baseball cards.

One of the most common "people" issues I've seen small business owners face is implementing a framework that defines where each team member is headed, how they will reach their next milestone, and what development is required to get there. This three-headed dragon can feel daunting. If you have a small organization of fewer than ten people, for example, it may feel like building the Taj Mahal for a tourist who is just stopping by for a photo.

In all my experience, I've never found time spent on career paths, training and development plans, and HR/leadership structure to be wasted. While balance is necessary, once you grow to twenty or more team members, these systems become imperative for reducing turnover, preventing burnout, and building a workforce that endures.

If you have the ability and time, consider evolving your organizational structure from the traditional '60s pyramid model to a matrix design. Envision your team as a latticework: People working within functional departments rather than reporting to a single person with dozens of direct reports. It's a "team of teams," interdependent and collaborative.

A few years ago, we did project work for one of the top 1% most successful wealth management firms in the U.S. From my perspective, they've succeeded despite having a strange and rigid culture. I've often thought they'd make a fascinating Harvard Business School case study. Their environment is micromanaged and cutthroat. As part of their process, each staff member is required to take ten consecutive days of vacation so their work can be audited in their absence. While the concept has merit, the execution feels inhumane. I often wonder how much more successful they might be, perhaps even the most successful, if their culture supported their team instead of undermining them.

FLATTENING YOUR ORGANIZATION

Top-heavy leadership structures almost always result in dysfunction. During my time as a department VP at a Fortune 200 firm, I sat through countless meetings where department heads were obsessed with increasing headcount and scope, because more people meant more budget and, consequently, greater perceived importance. But the traditional pyramid becomes self-serving and wasteful.

Employees respect leaders who've done the job, and even more so, those who are still doing it.

Flattening your organization and creating micro-leadership roles results in small teams within teams. In the NBA of the '60s and '70s, there was the concept of a "player-coach," someone who both played and coached. This is a powerful metaphor for business. Employees respect leaders who've done the job, and even more so, those who are still doing it.

In a matrix structure, individuals can make lateral moves within their function while taking on elevated responsibilities. A tenured team member can become a peer coach, adding marginal cost to the business while delivering tactical leadership rooted in experience, not just title.

Career paths should be tangible and actionable. Outline five or more milestones with potential increases in title, compensation, and responsibility. One common mistake entrepreneurs make is stretching promotion timelines over ten or more years. Whether we agree with it or not, the next generation expects speed and clarity.

As someone from a previous generation, I understand the long grind. Many founders took on debt, mopped floors, and did menial work despite owning the business. However, today's team members may feel stuck if they don't see meaningful progress within thirty-six months.

You can be right, or you can be effective. Being effective means adapting your systems to engage the next generation, drawing out their potential while grooming them to become future partners or successors.

In our chapter on the Potential Principle, we'll explore the three rungs of the ownership ladder. Not every team member needs to become a partner, and that's okay. Personally, I prefer businesses with few partners and many owners.

CAREER PATH

Career milestones can include a checklist of criteria for advancement. For today's workforce, motivation isn't just about money. It's about "Money, Marbles, and Chalk." Money is self-evident; your people are working in your business and expect to be compensated so that they can pay for the life they lead. Marbles are the accolades they receive in the form of trophies, trinkets, and hardware that sit on their desk; even company-branded gear and a Yeti can be endearing. Chalk is their name in lights, accolades in a group setting, or a team meeting that brings attention to their work and performance. It's wise to understand and learn what your people's motivators are. I'm finding more and more that with the next generation that we can't just assume a $5,000 bonus or a raise is going to garner loyalty and commitment. I guarantee that you currently have someone on your team who would take an extra day or two of vacation over that discretionary year-end check you plan to give them. Do you know who they are?

The best entrepreneurs treat career development like surgery. Minor tweaks and micro-movements can drastically improve your people leadership process. In this matrixed structure, I recommend you consider pivot roles, positions that enable people to switch career paths internally.

The company should retain the right to decide the timing of these moves. Team members may need to stay in a role for an additional eighteen months while preparations are made. This approach keeps transitions smooth, intentional, and symbiotic.

One best practice: Use a one-page "Career Lattice" to illustrate directional opportunities schematically. The acronym "WIIFM" (What's In It For Me?) is key here. What's powerful about the lattice is that it removes judgment: There are no "good" or "bad" paths, just different directions. Pairing this idea with clearly defined career paths gives individuals long-term clarity and real-time guidance.

Career Lattice

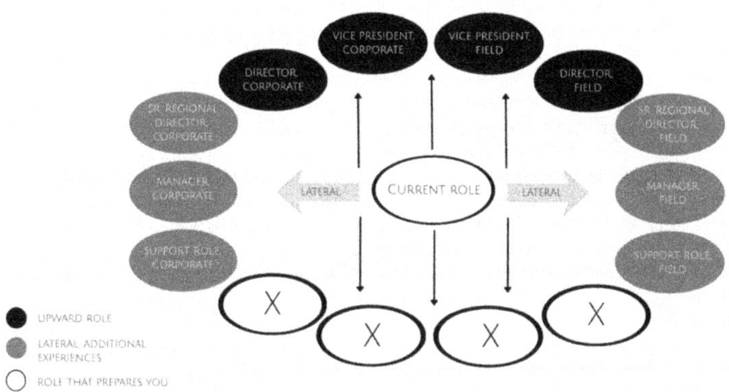

Figure 7: The Career Lattice

Career path design can come in many visual forms. Most I've seen are hierarchical, clinging to the macho assumptions of firms of the '60s and '70s: I'm above you; you're below me. In my humble opinion, a better way is a model that guides the viewer's eyes from left to right. We're conditioned to find comfort in this movement within the English language. We read from left to right, and when things feel familiar and comfortable, our guard is lowered and we become more open to the message. Here is a sample of how this comes together:

ADVISOR CAREER PATH REQUIREMENTS

Requirements	Associate Financial Advisor III	Associate Financial Advisor II	Lead Financial Advisor I
Minimum Years Experience	• 3+ years providing comprehensive planning	5+ years performing the duties of a Financial Planner	7+ years in the Financial Services Industry providing comprehensive financial planning
Education & Training	• 4-year degree; preferred in business, finance, accounting • Attends industry-related continuing education • Knowledge of planning software	• 4-year degree; preferred in business, finance, accounting • Attends continuing education • Proficient-planning software • VDP Training	• Attends substantial industry-related courses • Expertly uses financial planning software • SME in specific area
Certification & Designations	• Series 7, 66 (or 63 & 65) • State Life & Health and VA-Variable Life Insurance licenses	• APMA required • CFP, CPA, MBA or other related advanced designation is preferred	• CFP, CIMA or CFA (required), and other related advanced designation is required
Observations & Demonstrated Skills	• Developed advisor trust • Meet productivity plan metrics and strict deadlines • Exposure to investment chouces & their use	• Support advisors at client meetings • Apply understanding of investments • Mentors staff	• More highly involved in client meetings • Readily contribute knowledge as an SME for client meetings and Roundtable
Observations & Coaching by Practice Management Manager	• Complete plans as assigned with mentor oversight • Manage multiple projects & prioritize workflow • Complete reviews - if applicable	• Collaborates with advisors on plan completion	• Offers planning observations and advice
Demonstrated [YOUR COMPANY NAME]	• Roundtable attendance • Ed Day & other FA meetings	• Contributes during Roundtable • Education Day & other meetings	• Contributes during Roundtable • Education Day & other meetings
Position Requirements	• Complete Best Practices Projects • Participate in the greater good • Error-free plan with supporting analysis & file set up	• Proactively participate in the greater good • Error-free plan development, supporting analysis & file set up	• Proficiently in all aspects of position and specialty • Proactively participate in the greater good
Promotion Requirements	• CFP, CPA or MBA desirable • Securities, Insurance licenses • In good standing with all rules, regulations & policies	• CFP, CPA or MBA or other advances designations required • In good standing • 25 new accounts & 5mm assets gathered	• In good standing with all rules, regulations & policies • 100 new accounts & 50 mm assets gathered

Figure 8: Example Career Path Requirements

As we wrap up our People Principle, I'd like to share some experience related to a common question I've run into with entrepreneurs who are looking to manage the financial, capacity, and customer/client aspects of hiring and firing: *Is hiring another person the only answer?*

It can be paralyzing to think that the only answer to stress and strain on the team is to just throw another body at the problem: hire, hire, hire! This surely cannot be the only answer. As technology and efficiencies continue to influence all industries, better entrepreneurs recognize the importance of moving their human capital up the hourly pyramid and replacing the lowest hourly-value tasks with automation and technologies, like the advancements we see in AI. These entrepreneurs will win big.

If you picture a pyramid that includes all the individual tasks your team is responsible for, with the lowest-value tasks at the bottom and the highest-value tasks at the top, you'll understand why the task structure forms a pyramid. There are dozens upon dozens of "menial" tasks that need to be completed and require less skill. Conversely, there are fewer tasks at the top of the pyramid that demand greater skill and therefore command a premium hourly rate.

While the ideal entrepreneurial venture should not rely on being paid by the hour, this concept helps illustrate how you should allocate resources and expenditures to drive success. It's not only critical to remove discretion at the operating level (the bottom of the pyramid), but equally important to reduce the need for human capital at this lowest level, which is typically your greatest cost.

By leveraging automation and systems at the base of the pyramid, you can reduce human error, increase consistency, and free up your team to build skills and deliver more value as they move upward. This shift can take various forms, such as outsourcing tasks to lower-cost labor markets or engaging organizations that specialize in those functions at scale.

Innovations in artificial intelligence are especially intriguing. Just recently, I saw a firm outsource its initial interview screenings to AI. The AI interviewer handles the front-loaded, standard questions and due diligence on behalf of HR. This helps "weed out" unqualified candidates, allowing the HR professional to focus on the more nuanced and human aspects of the process. Some readers may be put off by this idea, but give it time. Think of all the innovations over the decades that once seemed radical and have now rendered previously "critical" tasks obsolete.

Taking a thoughtful, data-driven approach (what I often call a "math and science" lens) to your business, especially around capacity, people, and efficacy, can uncover insights that significantly improve outcomes and resource utilization.

ACCOUNTABILITY IN YOUR ECOSYSTEM

One critical tool we've found effective with the teams we coach is the time study.

The basic idea is for the entire team to go about their typical work during a standard business cycle, when most people are present, and document what they're doing throughout the day.

The best time studies:

- Categorize common activities based on team function.
- Require documentation of activities every thirty minutes throughout the workday.
- Provide clarity on how individual time is actually being spent.

Importantly, this is not a "keep your job" exercise. Messaging is key. If someone feels their role is under threat, they may fill their day with busywork that doesn't reflect a normal workflow.

When implemented properly, team members will accurately document what's really happening. The leadership team then takes accountability for the results. After all, the time study reflects the ecosystem created by leadership, not just individual behaviors.

In most cases, people act in ways that are tolerated. If someone is inefficient or focusing on the wrong tasks, they probably haven't received clear direction about their role or expectations.

If an individual can't describe what a successful day looks like or identify the key performance indicators (KPIs) that measure their productivity, that's a leadership failure, not just an employee oversight.

Occasionally, a time study may reveal that a role is no longer needed. If a role is eliminated, it should be because it no longer adds value to the ecosystem, not due to an individual's poor performance.

Ideally, the time study is facilitated by someone with benchmark data that can offer observations and recommendations for improvement.

If you're interested in conducting a time study, please scan the QR Code at the beginning or end of the book to learn more.

When an entrepreneur gets serious about their business, they recognize the power that is unlocked when they focus on designing and building the structure of their human capital, whether that's an organizational chart or an accountability chart.

Whether it's a command-and-control, top-down leadership style or a more matrixed and fractional leadership model, the important thing is to define the organizational structure and create clarity around who owns what.

When everyone owns it, no one does. One person must be accountable for each core function of the organization. Every seat on the team needs a clearly defined function, with roles and responsibilities. A title on a business card isn't enough.

Once the structure is outlined and seats are defined, you can assess what capabilities are needed in the individuals who fill those seats. Too many organizations rely on a "good ol' boy" system, based on tenure, relationships, and past performance, while trying to drive the business forward.

The best entrepreneurs I've worked with understand the critical nature of designing and leading their ecosystem. A time study is the starting point for evaluating whether a seat is functioning as intended. If it's not, either the seat needs to change, or the person in it does.

The best entrepreneurs I've worked with understand the critical nature of designing and leading their ecosystem.

Beyond system design and seat definition, there are also telltale signs that your business may need a new hire or a re-evaluation of your customer/client mix.

If you've strayed from your company's ideal market and started adding non-traditional or non-ideal customers/clients, dysfunction and inefficiency can arise. This stretches your team and your operating system.

If your strategy has intentionally shifted due to innovation or market changes, that's completely fine, but recognize the impact. You'll likely need to adapt your people and systems to support this new direction. That's a natural part of the growth journey. However, if you've unintentionally drifted in a new direction and the economics don't support it, it's time to course-correct. Get extreme clarity on who your ideal client or customer is.

In some cases, the best move may be to let clients go. This might involve selling those relationships (if viable in your industry) or letting them naturally attrite to competitors. Either way, your goal is to protect your ecosystem and right-size your customer base to align with your people, processes, and systems.

Remember: Growth for growth's sake is a fool's errand. It can become a prison, where you're held captive by your own success, and that success may silently undermine your intended strategy.

Not all success is created equal. A high volume of sales or customers may actually be counterproductive to your profit margins, team structure, or service quality.

This is how businesses lose momentum, culture, spirit, and ultimately, enterprise value.

As an entrepreneur, you must lead this evaluation. My goal is to motivate you to take a clear, hard look at your company's strategy. Let's hack at the root, not just treat the symptoms.

Human capital challenges almost always reflect either:

- A lack of strategic intentionality by leadership, or
- A tolerance of behaviors, enabled by a dysfunctional ecosystem.

Leaders must own both: the strategy and the ecosystem. When both are understood and aligned, business performance and customer experience become consistent, and that's how you win.

THE 5 SIGNS IT'S TIME TO HIRE OR FIRE

If, in your analysis of the business, you find that:

- The strategy is on track
- Leadership has built a healthy ecosystem with strong controls and culture
- People are progressing up the pyramid of task vs. hourly rate

... and yet you're still experiencing strain on your human capital, it may be time to evaluate "The 5 Signs It's Time to Hire or Fire." Years ago, I published this framework on our blog. It has proven invaluable for leadership teams, helping them gain the confidence to navigate uncertainty and make smarter decisions about when to hire and when not to.

Keep in mind: The house has to be in order first. The ailments outlined in the 5 Signs may be symptoms of deeper root causes, such as:

- Strategy drift
- A dysfunctional internal ecosystem

These must be your starting points. Once you're confident in your pursuit and servicing of your ideal clients/customers, and your systems support the right people in the right seats, you're ready to leverage the final litmus test.

The 5 Signs It's Time to Hire or Fire helps you assess whether it's time to bring on new team members or prune your client/customer portfolio. This is not just about staffing—it's about maintaining the health of your business ecosystem.

On the following page, you can see the circular nature of this challenge in business: Each of the 5 Signs impacts the others. The 5 Signs are:

- Number of customers/clients per servicer
- A low capacity to take on new customers/clients (business slowing)
- Consistent requests for or utilization of overtime (work extending beyond normal business hours typical to your company)
- Complaints from the team about workload (a little sleuthing may reveal that members of your team have their résumés posted on job sites)
- Missed deadlines for service or product delivery (a key indicator that your quality is declining)

Vineyard owners must be meticulous in maintaining the plants in the field. When a fruit tree or grapevine is allowed to overgrow its base and roots, the quality of the fruit declines and sometimes even sours. To sustain a healthy orchard or vineyard, the caretaker must prune, trim, and evaluate regularly. The discipline of the landowner and of the plants that generate the yield is what ensures long-term success.

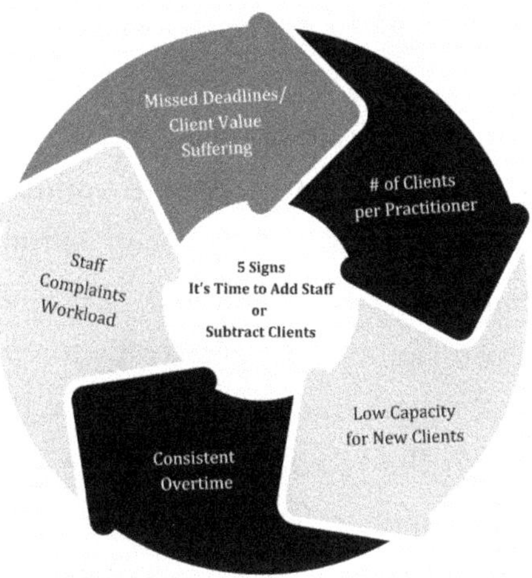

Figure 9: 5 Signs It's Time to Add Staff or Subtract Clients

In the same way, the entrepreneur must continually evaluate the scale and quality of the clients and customers in the business. That's why I've designed the 5 Signs framework to offer a holistic view, encompassing both the internal support team and human capital and the external end users: your clients and customers. Without seeing both sides of the coin, a business owner risks making tactical hiring decisions that only treat symptoms, not root causes.

This framework is intended to begin with a key indicator that we'll explore more deeply in the chapter on the fourth principle: Profit. That indicator is the number of customers or clients per servicing unit. Since this book is designed to be universally applicable, a "servicing unit" may look different in your industry compared to another reader's.

What we aim to measure is the individual, team, or department responsible for providing ongoing service to your existing customer or client base. By calculating the number of clients per servicing unit, you can establish a baseline. In some cases, your industry may already offer benchmarks for businesses of similar size or revenue.

Personally, I'm a firm believer that good decisions are based on good data. This is simple, perhaps even fundamental, but it's a truth that serves every business owner well. While gut instinct and experience should not be dismissed, as your business and industry evolve, you cannot rely solely on what you've seen in the rearview mirror. A strong dataset and reliable benchmarks allow you to look through the windshield and see around the corners ahead.

If you don't have a benchmark or comparison point, your best option is to build your own dataset. A bit of historical digging can help you establish a three-year trend as a starting point. From there, you can analyze whether the current pressure you're feeling around this key indicator has always existed or if it's a new and emerging trend.

The second key indicator to consider is a low capacity for new customer or client acquisition. Is your team struggling to meet quotas? Having trouble onboarding? Do you hear complaints or hesitation when a new client is coming on?

For the types of businesses I specialize in, the root cause behind symptoms like these usually comes down to two things:

- A lack of clarity around the ideal client/customer
- A lack of discipline in how the entrepreneur has managed the ecosystem (the "vineyard," in the earlier analogy)

If you haven't yet segmented your client/customer base into two or three tiers, each with varying levels of service and resource allocation, now is the time. This kind of strategic segmentation is often at the root of many of the 5 Signs (or symptoms) in this process.

In many businesses, the team responsible for acquiring the client is not the same team responsible for servicing them. This structure can present challenges, such as the business development team bringing in less-than-ideal clients just to hit quotas. Nevertheless, it can be even more problematic when the same team is responsible for both acquisition and service.

While the thrill of landing a new client is exciting and often tied to compensation and incentives, the pain of onboarding and servicing that new client can become a counter-motivator. Even when cash incentives are properly aligned, the cumulative burden of "just one more" client can lead to a slowdown in new client generation.

The third key indicator is a consistent or constant request for overtime. If your employees are salaried, you'll want to look for signs that they're regularly working beyond industry norms: late nights, weekends, holidays, or missed days off.

Entrepreneurs often appreciate team members who are dedicated, go-getters, and willing to go the extra mile for the sake of the business or the customer. But as the saying goes, too much of a good thing is still too much.

Overwork leads to fatigue, which can lead to resentment toward you, the business, or even the customers. If your team is stretched too thin, the symptoms will eventually show up in:

- Turnover
- Mistakes
- Declining morale and culture

As with the other indicators, having historical data and industry benchmarks will help you determine whether this is a short-term fluctuation or a deeper, systemic issue.

That said, not all overtime is created equal. If the need stems from inefficiency, poor time management, or perfectionism, then that's a different challenge. What we're talking about here is when your best people consistently can't complete their responsibilities within a normal, expected timeframe, even when they're performing at a high level. There's nothing wrong with an intermittent or episodic need for a "push" of activity due to a major project or a critical need for a customer/client. But this should be the exception, not the norm. I refer to your best people because they are the litmus test or standard to which you want the entire organization to operate, at a minimum, to strive for. When those you feel represent your brand best are constantly on pace to work overtime, you have a problem. The odds of a breakdown in your system, productivity, or the individual themselves increase exponentially the longer you allow this to go unaddressed. I've seen the best people on a team dragged down to below average, all due to the business owner's unwillingness or unawareness that they are draining their people. The saying goes that "pigs get fat and hogs get slaughtered." A crude saying, perhaps, but it illustrates the point that a wise entrepreneur recognizes the value that their best people provide, and they're willing to protect and invest in them by not expecting more than is reasonable over the long run.

Our fourth indicator is ongoing complaints about workload. Occasional, intermittent complaints are not a problem: Everyone vents from time to time. But constant or consistent grumbling is a red flag. Everyone has days when they feel stretched thin or need to vent. But when complaints about workload become a pattern rather than an exception, it signals a deeper issue. Chronic grumbling suggests that the team is operating beyond its sustainable capacity. When people feel perpetually overloaded, their mental bandwidth narrows, creativity drops, and small challenges start to feel insurmountable.

Leaders often misread this as a morale problem when it's actually a structural one. It means you've likely hit (or exceeded) the natural limits of your current staffing or client load. The noise you hear is your team's way of saying, "We can't keep this up." At this point, one of two things must happen: You either hire additional help or right-size your client base. If you don't, you risk burnout, turnover, and declining quality in your client experience.

Healthy teams discuss workload with solutions in mind; unhealthy ones complain because they've lost confidence that change is coming. The difference between those two outcomes is leadership's willingness to listen and act.

It's remarkable how some individuals have an extremely high tolerance for pain and pressure. They can endure a lot. However, the best entrepreneurs are sensitive to this and understand that endurance should not be exploited over years or decades. You simply won't get the best results when you take advantage of someone's ability to endure hardship.

The fifth and final indicator that it may be time to hire new staff or let go of clients is a decline in service or product quality, as well as missed deadlines. If your team is struggling to maintain the quality and standards that your reputation was built on, the consequences can be cascading. This decline often leads to customer dissatisfaction, internal frustration, and even loss of business.

Now, if the dip in performance is due to new processes, new team members, or external disruptions, that's a different situation altogether. What we're focusing on here is when a long-standing team, working under normal business conditions, suddenly begins to struggle with tasks they've historically handled well. If there are no external factors, then you're likely dealing with one of the 5 Signs.

As you and your leadership team begin to assess and examine the problem, I've found these five indicators to be an effective framework for accurately diagnosing the root issue.

Once you've identified the one or two most pressing indicators, the next step is to determine the true root cause:

- Is it a lack of human capital resources, requiring a new hire?
- Or have you drifted from your ideal client strategy, and your vineyard needs pruning?

As author Jim Collins famously observed, great companies share two key characteristics (among others): disciplined people and disciplined decision-making. My hope is that these five indicators will be as valuable for you as they have been for me in uncovering the true issues and helping you effectively hack at the root, rather than merely trimming the branches!

PRINCIPLE 3: PROCESS

You might think that, for the Process Principle, we would begin with insights from my Six Sigma Black Belt training and experience. And yes, you will see those elements woven in as we explore how the best entrepreneurs drive efficiency and implement error-reduction methodologies. However, before diving into tools and systems, we need to talk about leadership.

In the end, leadership matters. The most impactful people I've worked with, whether they held formal titles or not, were exceptional leaders. There are countless books on the subject, each offering its own insights. We hear phrases like: "Leaders eat last." "Leadership is doing the right things; management is doing things right." "Leadership is taking people to places they couldn't or wouldn't go on their own." The list goes on.

For me, the most inspiring leaders are those who lead with humility. Whether it's shown through a bit of self-deprecating humor or a willingness to admit a weakness or lack of skill compared to their peers, humble leaders are the ones who endure

—the ones who are admired and remembered long after they're gone.

For me, the most inspiring leaders are those who lead with humility.

Unfortunately, in politics, entertainment, and the media we consume, we're often presented with a counterfeit version of leadership, as we discussed earlier in the principle of Purpose. These false leaders may use tactics like self-deprecating humor or admitting faults, not from a place of authenticity, but as a means to manipulate or ingratiate. It's subtle, and many people today don't even recognize it.

PROCESS IS SYMBIOTIC WITH HUMILITY

I fear we've lost our way in our ability to identify and develop humble leaders. Self-aggrandizement is often cloaked in the guise of a "humble brag." Influencers, spiritual figures, or movement leaders are frequently portrayed alongside material wealth, held up as proof of their success. In today's world, we've put a price tag on leadership. Millionaire is the first rung; billionaire is the top of the ladder.

Society has an insatiable appetite for flash, glamour, and the fame that wealth brings. But true leaders see money not as the measure of success but as a tool: a means of leveraging their purpose, passion, or cause. Rare are the leaders like Mahatma Gandhi, who inspire lasting, authentic change.

And yes, Gandhi is a high bar. But let's be clear: The small business owner reading or listening to this book doesn't need to abandon their business, hand-stitch their own clothes, or go on a hunger strike. What I'm referring to is a leader who is grounded in who they are and aware of who they are not.

They are anchored in a purpose greater than themselves that, while often expressed through a capitalistic venture, has a positive impact on thousands. Entrepreneurs are the bedrock of free economies, and whether that purpose is to feed the casual stroller on a city sidewalk, delight a child with an inventive toy, or improve global health and well-being, it is this fire that fuels others to follow and act.

Both consumers and employees, the thousands touched by the entrepreneur's vision, are given:

- Meaningful work
- Income to sustain life
- Opportunities to invest in their future
- And in some cases, a path to generational wealth where none existed before.

As we turn our attention to the Process Principle, keep in mind: Leadership is the current running through it all. The most successful entrepreneurs recognize that a process or system becomes symbiotic with the guidance of a humble leader.

Processes and procedures are not just operational tools; they are the guardians and enforcers of the leader's culture.

Take, for example, the story of the Venetians. Forced from mainland Italy around the turn of the eighteenth century, they were compelled by existential threat to create a new city-state. Out of necessity and ingenuity, they drove wooden pylons into the clay beds of marshy, disconnected islands, laying the foundation for what would become Venice. Over time, and even to this day, those original pylons support a city beloved by all who visit.

In the same way, strong leadership rooted in humility and purpose lays the foundation. And over time, with intentional processes and systems, it supports a business that others admire, believe in, and want to be part of.

If the essence of Venice is the culture of your business, then the pylons of your leadership are the processes and systems we will discuss now. Is it a lofty analogy? Perhaps. But the visualization of how leadership, culture, and process intersect should help the reader inspect their current environment and seek either confirmation or compulsion for change.

MANAGE SYSTEMS, NOT PEOPLE

Let's start with a fundamental truth that my coaching team and I preach daily: The best leaders MANAGE SYSTEMS, NOT PEOPLE.

"Manager" is a title I've disagreed with for a couple of decades now. It feels like an antiquated descriptor that conjures images of someone arriving at work and having to report to a superior. "Management" refers to a group of these titled individuals within a hierarchical framework, outlining who's the boss and where employees should go for help with problems, personnel issues, or pay.

I wish there were a more accurate, modern descriptor for this role, but for now, "manager" remains the universal term for the guy or gal in charge.

When we say "manage systems, not people," what we really mean is that people need leadership, not control.

Process has everything to do with people. People are emotional, dynamic beings. When we say "manage systems, not people," what we really mean is that people need leadership, not control.

Leadership, in turn, is built on the pylons of structure, process, procedures, and systems. It's rare for someone to have a lasting impact on a business without having systems in place. The most effective entrepreneurs I've worked with understand the interconnected relationship between leadership, systems, and people.

So, let's break down the key principles that bring together the leadership of people and the management of systems.

PEOPLE EMBRACE WHAT THEY DISCOVER

One foundational truth: People embrace what they discover. If I'm told, I might understand. But if I discover it, I adopt it.

For lasting change, leaders must create space within the ecosystem to allow discovery. This means extending some grace for mistakes, especially those that don't harm a client or others. In fact, such mistakes are often invaluable learning moments.

As you reflect on your current team and ecosystem, ask yourself:

- How much of the second CQ (the Curiosity Quotient) is being leveraged for learning and discovery?
- Where can people be allowed to truly be people?

Is your training process overly rigid and command-and-control driven? Does it lean too much on "show and tell," leaving team members feeling like compliance is the only path to survival and that they're just another cog in the wheel?

Certainly, there are basics in your business where discretion should be removed. A "see ball, hit ball" approach is necessary in some operational areas. But the training process should also provide space for the learner to be left to their own devices—to experience the value of self-discovery.

When we learn something for ourselves, we don't need a witness. The principle becomes self-evident, and we gain deep conviction in its value. We're not encouraging third-degree burns here, but if you've ever touched a hot stove, even for a split second, you know the lesson is imprinted for life. So, what are you doing in your business to foster curiosity, discovery, and learning?

There's also tremendous value in involving the people who will use the system in its design. Just as we embrace what we discover, we also embrace what we help build. One major benefit for the leader in building from the "bottom up" is that the builder gains a sense of accountability to the system they helped create.

Imagine you have a team member named Susan who has experienced some performance issues. Despite this, Susan brings critical skills and behaviors to the table, skills you value and that she executes consistently and accurately.

However, your business is evolving rapidly due to technological advancements, often requiring process tweaks or even complete system overhauls. Recently, your firm rolled out a new client relationship management (CRM) platform. It's a modern, powerful tool. Like any new tech, it has a few bugs, but adoption is critical for long-term success.

Susan plays a central role in using this CRM. And as you may have guessed, she's struggling with the change.

You have a few options:

- You could mandate immediate compliance using a command-and-control, show-and-tell approach, possibly backed by the threat of a performance improvement plan.
- But we both know where that path often leads. If Susan digs in her heels, chances are, you'll dig in yours.

If we embrace the idea of managing systems, not people, the wise entrepreneur will involve Susan in the solution. She becomes one of your builders.

Susan's role in the build, if she lacks prior project leadership experience, may be in a support or sounding board capacity. We're not looking to set her up to fail but to help her win. We want and appreciate Susan's involvement in the process. That's critical to long-term success.

In the teams I coach, we talk about this concept frequently. Some teams even formalize this model as part of their organization. If your team is large enough, you can add what we call working groups.

This concept isn't new: it's an adaptation of Kelly Johnson's Skunk Works program from Lockheed Martin. During the Cold War, the U.S. required rapid innovation in avionics at a pace never seen before. Think Orville and Wilbur Wright-level breakthroughs, but now in jet propulsion and aerodynamics. Skunk Works brought together elite personnel from across the organization to solve mission-critical problems. These working groups could last days or months, however long it took.

Jeff Bezos might reference his "two-pizza rule" here: small, agile teams that can be fed with two pizzas (or, for entrepreneurs, maybe just half a pizza!).

When implementing this model in your business, I recommend being transparent. Don't keep it a secret. Introduce the concept openly. Let your team know it's here to stay. Invite volunteers along the way, but be clear: final selections rest with leadership.

The working group model fosters curiosity, ownership, and accountability.

Let's return to our example of Susan. By placing her in a support or leadership role within the working group, she becomes an architect of the system. She now embraces what she helped build and becomes an advocate for its adoption, enhancement, and long-term success.

Will there still be resistance? Possibly. We all resist change to some degree. But Susan will take pride in her contribution, and that makes her far more likely to say "yes" to change.

This is a win-win. Most importantly, the entrepreneur has channeled energy in a way that builds both the business and its culture.

WILLING PARTICIPANTS, NOT HOSTAGES

Now let's flash forward six months. Susan has a relapse; she's struggling again. But because she helped design the system, you now have a powerful tool for leading through the challenge. Rather than managing Susan, you return to managing the system. You might say, "Susan, we're consistently seeing a less-than-desirable outcome in this area. You were a key contributor to this system's design. Can we review the issues together and identify what might need to be modified?" This isn't manipulation; it's curiosity-driven leadership.

If the system has been stress-tested, and the process, procedure, and policy all check out, then it becomes clear the issue lies not in the system, but in execution.

Most performance reviews become a "he said, she said" scenario, relying too heavily on positional authority. Even with good intentions, your chances of success are slim if you're managing the person instead of the system. Instead, let the system be the benchmark.

This brings us to what I call the "trunk of agreement." Imagine two people out on opposite limbs of a tree, each clinging to their own perspective, data, and emotions. The only way forward is to climb back toward the trunk, to find common ground. That "trunk" might be a shared purpose, core values, or, in this case, the agreed-upon system.

When people realize that the system was well-designed, especially because they helped build it, they're more willing to accept that the problem lies in their own execution. That's where true change happens: when discovery is owned by the individual, not imposed by leadership.

And the result? The person doing the discovery becomes a willing participant, not a hostage.

That's powerful leadership.

FINAL THOUGHTS ON PROCESS

Let's be honest: Process can be maddening. System design often feels like a never-ending project. Just when you think you've nailed it, something changes.

In the Entrepreneurial Operating System (EOS), it's recommended that you document only the 20% of processes that impact 80% of your business. That sounds simple, but identifying that 20% can be challenging. A great starting point is to ask each department leader to define what is mission-critical.

And always remember this: The value you provide *is* your system. That applies to both your end users and your internal team.

Your culture lives and dies by process. No process? No culture. No culture? You've got chaos.

Too many teams rely on tribal knowledge: what lives in people's heads. The founder becomes the brain of the operation, and the more indispensable they are, the more dangerous it becomes for the company's future.

The foolish entrepreneur enjoys being "the one who knows everything." But their ego slowly kills the company.

You must document the tribal knowledge that runs your business. If your system is your value, why not name it and trademark it? The Entrepreneurial Operating System (EOS) recommends calling it your company's "WAY" (e.g., *The Acme Way*™). When you do this, the process becomes sacred. It becomes the foundation of your culture.

Well-documented processes serve as the standard against which your team can self-discover and self-manage.

In my experience, most people's problems stem from poorly designed systems. When there are no clear rules of engagement, people are forced to make decisions in emotional moments or, worse, follow directives from a "black box" with no visibility.

Take compensation plan design, for example. My team does a lot of work in this area. It's complex. And even when you land on a good plan, someone is bound to be unhappy. That's why I recommend starting every system, especially compensation plans, with a philosophy: What do you believe? Many entrepreneurs value meritocracy: rewards based on performance, not just tenure. Sure, you need market analysis (which we provide in all our comp design projects), but in most entrepreneurial organizations, compensation should reflect contribution, not just title or time served.

Your leadership improves when you engage your team in developing your Process principle.

So when building your *[Your Firm Name] Way*, start with principles, and then document thoughtful processes and procedures. Your leadership improves when you engage your team in developing your Process principle.

Strong operations teams follow a consistent documentation method. Use a standardized template with a structure like:

- Purpose
- Prerequisites
- Procedure

There's a QR code in the front and back of this book, which links to a sample template we provide to our coaching clients. It helps them document core systems clearly and consistently.

Avoid creating a physical manual. That might have worked in the '90s, but today, it's obsolete. In a fast-changing technological environment, the physical manual is a dinosaur.

Instead, use a cloud-based platform that allows you to:

- Document in real time
- Make live updates
- Keep processes accessible and actionable

The template we provide is not meant to be a static Word document you save, print, or share. It's a framework for structuring your process documentation within an online portal.

Your procedures should contain enough fundamentals for the user to confidently follow and execute. You create real value when a new hire off the street can step in and do what's intended. But beware of over-documentation. It can suffocate the intended value and lead to mutiny: not an open rebellion, but a quiet, passive resistance to following the documented process.

An effective operations leader will bring people into the tent and make them part of the solution.

Identify SMEs (subject matter experts) in your business. These individuals can:

- Keep procedures concise and focused
- Reinforce the *why* behind the process
- Drive adoption and accountability

YOUR TEAM MEETINGS ARE TERRIBLE

Let's be honest: Your team meetings are terrible. Well, maybe not *terrible*, but they're likely suboptimal. A common entrepreneurial mistake is doing the bare minimum with staff, team, and sales meetings. The experience is often one of three things:

- A root canal
- A three-ring circus
- A sermon from a tired, no-longer-passionate preacher

Believe me, I know. I've been a part of, or led, a version of all three at some point in my professional career.

So what is to be done? Let's start with some tips that can help you formulate a plan. First, we must be aware of intensity and frequency. The impact of these two concepts makes all the difference in the nature and regularity of your formal interactions with the team, particularly in one-on-one settings. Most entrepreneurs I work with have developed into dominant personalities, especially within their teams. Without intention, the business owner can be intimidating to most members of their team. This intimidation factor can be dialed up tenfold in a one-on-one setting. Their perception is your reality. Being cognizant of where you stand and the individual's experience with you is imperative if you are to win people over.

If the intensity of the meeting you are having is high, then the frequency of that interaction should be low. Too many leaders have a weekly one-on-one that grinds people up and spits them out. On a scale from 1 to 10, the anxiety is an 11, and the value the leader perceives they're creating is actually having the opposite result. Unless the individual on your team is new to their role (within the first twelve months), my experience tells me that a weekly formal one-on-one is too much unless the intensity of that one-on-one is dialed down. If it is less structured and a check-in for thirty minutes or less, weekly may be just fine.

If the team member is in an executive role (C-suite), chances are someone else is preparing data for review, so the intensity may be higher. But for middle management or other members of the team not in direct control of the business, treat the time you have with them with extreme care. Remember: intensity and frequency.

For your team meetings, I've found no better solution than the EOS Level 10 meeting. The structure, cadence, and pace are about as good as it gets for executive leadership or departmental meetings. There is real power in keeping the conversation on track with clarity of topic, no allowance for tangential or off-topic sidebars, and a collection of issues to discuss, once accountability, reporting, and updates have been completed. Ninety minutes of appropriately paced facilitation is an excellent experience for all in the room.

My safety tip would be this: When conducting team meetings (or any meeting for that matter), manage the meeting to content, not to time. If you can end a meeting early and have accomplished its objective, do it.

Another best practice that, when run well, can be a keeper of the culture is the daily stand-up meeting. This can be done when everyone is physically in the same space or when you have a virtual team spread across time zones with limits. Your team in India may have a difficult time doing a stand-up with your team in Canada, but a modification can allow you to do a daily stand-up within geographical limits.

The best daily STAND-UP meetings I've seen have the following characteristics:

S **Short & Structured:** – Keep it under ten minutes. Frequent cadence means you don't need depth here, just rhythm and efficiency.

T **Time & Agenda:** Same time, same agenda, every day. Routine builds trust and predictability.

A **Alignment with Values:** Begin by centering on a team value or principle to orient everyone to true north.

N **No Sitting:** Everyone stands. Standing increases focus and prevents lingering.

D **Distributed Load:** Different members of the team share responsibility for facilitating different components.

-

U **Update on Capacity:** Each member declares their workload (a simple "1–10" scale works here).

P **Priority Information:** Share the critical info for the day. Owners speak sparingly so that when they do, it's impactful.

There are some great attributes outlined above that can apply to any of your team meetings. If the intensity of your daily stand-ups is lower due to their frequency, then the intensity of your full-team meetings, if held monthly, might increase. This can be a time when you're reviewing company results YTD, addressing a critical initiative or imperative for the firm, or having departmental leaders "on the spot" to showcase what's happening in their part of the business. The idea here is that people need to come with their A-game.

For most team meetings, using the same agenda with key elements that need to be reviewed or updated makes the most sense. I've seen teams that play upbeat music before the meeting begins. Some start with a "joke of the day" from a team member who can deliver a punchline like a stand-up comedian. Others open with an inspirational quote or story, just like Paul Harvey used to do. Ultimately, your meetings need to be thoughtful, impactful, and part of your culture.

If you are in need of an upgrade, be purposeful about it. Don't just show up one day blasting Guns N' Roses and think that's going to make all the difference. Involve the team; do a blind survey if it makes sense, but don't disorient everyone. Bring them into the tent and let them know your meetings need a facelift, and then make it happen.

DEMONSTRATE, OBSERVE, CONFIRM

A final tip on meeting upgrades: Follow the simple training mode of DOC—demonstrate, observe, and confirm. If you're looking for a change, demonstrate what you're aiming for, observe your "trainee," provide feedback to assist in their success, and confirm that the result is what you wanted. Don't just expect a memo to make this happen. You must lead the process.

Another area I find most businesses lacking in is the impact and importance of business planning. For most firms, the business planning process has become mundane. Just a reprojection of numbers with a growth rate slapped on the data, and the spreadsheet updated. Voilà, business planning!

Don't get me wrong, there is value in growth rates, projections, and forecasts. But if the team isn't involved, if the process is driven almost exclusively top-down, you've missed the point.

Business planning should be inclusive. Every team member should feel a sense of ownership in the process, both in the short term (the next thirty-six months) and the long term (ten years or more). I view these as two parallel tracks that can run side by side.

Business planning should be inclusive. Every team member should feel a sense of ownership in the process.

Ultimately, the outcome we're aiming for is a living plan that is realistic, values-driven, and embraced at every level of the business. You know the planning process has been successful when frontline workers feel heard, department leaders gain clarity, and executives reinforce the vision, all while keeping both the three-year roadmap and ten-year destination alive in the company culture.

There are defined roles for each layer of the organization:

- **Front-line Workers are the Reality Checkers:** They provide critical operational insights, identify pain points, and offer real customer feedback.
- **Department Leaders are the Translators:** They connect the high-level vision to department-specific execution, ensuring strategies turn into results.
- **Owners/Executives are the Vision Holders:** They frame the "why" and define "where we're going," while creating space for others to help shape the "how."

SHORT-TERM AND LONG-TERM BUSINESS PLANNING

Here are a few safety tips and best practices that can significantly enhance your business planning process:

Track 1: Short-Term Planning (Thirty-six Months or Less)

- Purpose: Drive traction, accountability, and near-term priorities.
- Keep the time horizon realistic (no more than three years).
- Strategy translates into actionable quarterly and annual goals.
- Involve department leaders as coauthors of goals and front-line workers as reality-checkers. Projects should last 90-180 days with clear deliverables.
- Keep communication simple and repeatable: Everyone should be able to state the three-year picture in plain language.

The Short-Term Planning Checklist

- Conduct department listening sessions before planning. These can be collaborative or via a blind survey to get real feedback.
- Review and update the three-year business plan from last year. This shifts annually. For example, if this year's three-year plan ends in 2030, next year's should end in 2031.
- Define annual priorities (one-year plan) that are imperatives to achieve the three-year markers. The "math" should logically jump from this year to three years from now.
- Break annual priorities into twelve quarterly project lists. EOS calls these projects or tasks ROCKS.
- Assign clear ownership for each project or rock. Ideally, a project has a weekly update and thirteen milestones

in a thirteen-week quarter. Reality is rarely perfect, but ten milestones per quarter keep you on track.

- Don't miss the capacity check: Are resources aligned with goals? Too often, leadership signs up for initiatives not vetted against available time, tools, and people. Ask the doers, "Can we actually do this?" If they say no, it deserves due diligence. Sometimes front-liners underestimate their capability, and sometimes they're right. A good entrepreneur navigates the difference.
- EOS has a great document called the Vision/Traction Organizer (VTO) that summarizes the plan on one page. At a minimum, review the plan every 180 days to check traction.
- Cascade the plan in department/team meetings so everyone knows their role in achieving success.
- Schedule quarterly business reviews (QBRs) with leaders and rotating frontline reps to join special projects. This serves two purposes: (1) managers often know less than front-liners, so key details aren't missed, and (2) it's a leadership development opportunity for front-liners to gain exposure and demonstrate skill.

Track 2: Long-Term Planning (10+ Years)

- Purpose: Define vision, legacy, and cultural trajectory.
- Encourage aspirational, future-oriented thinking, not just operational fixes.
- Before involving the executive leadership team, engage a diverse mix of leaders and employees. Front-line voices can inspire powerful long-term direction. (If you plan a small-group session, use a skilled facilitator to keep the meeting on track and avoid false promises.)

- Use storytelling and visualization (mock-ups, metaphors, legacy statements) to make the Ten-Year Target tangible.
- Revisit long-term goals annually, but keep the vision steady; stability builds confidence.

The Long-Term Planning Checklist

- Host an annual "envisioning" workshop or retreat with your executive team. Pre-work should include collecting aspirational ideas from the broader team. Ask, "What do we want this company to look like in ten years?"
- Ground the document in company values, purpose, cause, and passion. The ten-year target should be simple, bold, and a little uncomfortable.
- Confirm the Ten-Year Target. Don't adjust it unless there's a major industry shift, leadership/ownership change, or extraordinary opportunity. If the target keeps evolving, the team will just wait for clarity instead of acting.
- Validate that core values and purpose remain relevant. These rarely change. Pulse check: Ask employees if they see the company living out its values and where alignment is slipping.
- Bring the Ten-Year Plan to life. Document stories that reinforce values and long-term aspirations. Create visuals/mock-ups of the vision (not just words).
- Ensure ownership communicates vision consistently at all levels. Cascade long-term goals into departmental vision sessions. Transparency is key: always "close the loop" by showing how input shaped the plan.

- Demystify strategy: Translate corporate vision into plain language so every level can engage meaningfully.
- Establish a communication rhythm: Use quarterly meetings for short-term traction and annual retreats for long-term vision.
- Balance the voices: Owners set the vision, leaders translate it, and workers ground the plan in reality.
- Recognize contributions: Highlight employee input that shaped goals or vision, and provide tangible proof of inclusion. Always share back what you heard, what made it into the plan, and why. Transparency builds trust.
- Keep it a living document: Display the ten-year plan daily.
- A great story comes from NASA. When President JFK asked a janitor what he was working on, the janitor replied, "I'm helping put a man on the moon." That's how you want your team to see and experience the ten-year vision.

So, what is the result of a dual-track business planning system?

You get the best of everyone's efforts to bring the two together. The players on the field understand their roles in the planning process, short-term execution is laser-focused, and long-term vision is inspiring and stable, with both leaders and front-line employees meaningfully involved. You know you've achieved greatness in the business planning process when you've empowered leaders and front-liners to lead parts of the process. This can be accomplished by rotating facilitation of portions of planning sessions (e.g., the department leader facilitates SWOT analyses, and frontline workers share client perspectives).

Lastly, the owners should speak sparingly but powerfully. Your role as the business owner in the process is to reinforce "why we exist" and the long-term vision while avoiding dominating discussions. When your team self-discovers and creates, they become the solution to any problem and will do any given *how* to achieve the *why*.

LEADERSHIP OF THE PROCESS PRINCIPLE

When thinking about the leadership of the Process Principle within your business, it becomes clear that the people leading the process are critical. Once your organization has grown beyond twenty employees, you're starting to reach a point where the Triangle Offense of Operations may suit you well.

I'm a big fan of the '90s Chicago Bulls franchise of the NBA. *The Last Dance* chronicles many things I didn't know about the dynasty, but what I was very aware of from the early stages of the Bulls' run was the institution of the Triangle Offense. For those who aren't basketball fans, the Triangle Offense was a system refined and popularized by Hall of Fame coach Tex Winter. The concept is that three of the five offensive players on the court work in tandem as the ball swings from one side of the court to the other, fluidly creating open shots to score.

A few elements of the Triangle Offense that apply in business include:

- Each player plays a position and has a spot on the floor they aim to get to.
- Each player has a specialty on offense that the system seeks to exploit.
- Teamwork makes the dream work: They must collaborate and get to their spot to be most effective.

The business application? In operations, it's extremely rare to find a leader who has a mind for strategy, is fantastic at systems and process design, and is great with people. When you do find this triple threat, do everything you can to keep them.

If your team hasn't found that unicorn, then leverage the triple threat as a composite of different contributors. You, as the entrepreneur, may have to play the strategist role if you don't yet have that person on your executive team (typically a COO or Director of Operations). To support that individual, identify two other members, even if only in fractional roles, as the people leader and the systems leader.

So, the triangle consists of

- The Strategist
- The People Leader
- The Systems Leader

Triangle Offense

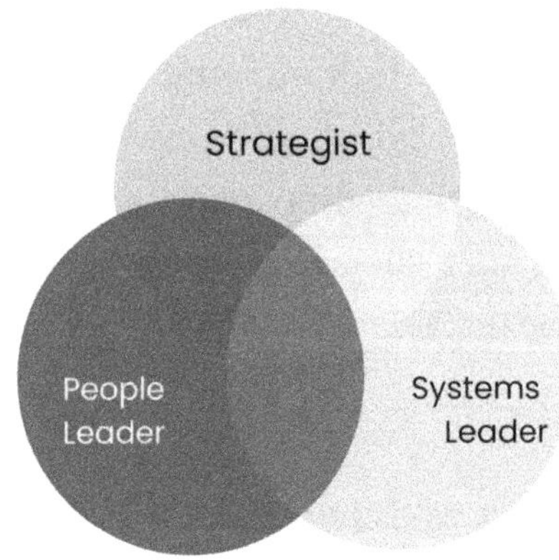

This trifecta of operations leads to incredibly successful outcomes. My whitepaper on this system is available on our website if you want to dive deeper into the what and how of the strategy (www.balanceapproach.com).

In the end, your People Leader can facilitate career path and development conversations, and your Systems Leader can facilitate training and ensure compliance. By having a clear point of view and a few key components to manage your systems, processes don't need to be feared or dreaded by your team. You'll gain confidence that you have a plan, and the process will take care of itself.

Your culture lives or dies based on the systems and processes you build to keep it alive and healthy. For many operations teams, a core part of that culture is a five- to seven-minute daily stand-up. This meeting can happen in person or virtually. Each day, the team gathers briefly to build camaraderie, share updates, react to last-minute calendar changes, and assess individual capacity.

Your culture lives or dies based on the systems and processes you build to keep it alive and healthy.

As a leader, I've found this kind of start to the day invaluable. I get a real-time pulse on the day's challenges, and, just as importantly, I can read body language and tone to spot who's good to go and who might need a personal check-in.

The best entrepreneurial organizations I've seen also include a quick, daily grounding in the firm's values or service standards. You might ask, "But really, every day?" Yes, every day. Having team members take turns reminding the group of our beliefs and standards, and the importance of living them out, can dramatically shape culture over time.

Even the mighty Mississippi and Nile rivers start with one drop of water. Your daily drip on your culture, through a short, structured stand-up, keeps momentum moving in the right direction. Leadership matters, and your care and attention to process matter just as much.

Now, onto the Profit Principle...

PRINCIPLE 4: PROFIT

I have assumed in writing this book that the reader is in a for-profit business. Of course, the other principles we have covered and will cover are highly applicable in both for-profit and non-profit organizations. However, for this chapter, you'll get the most value if you're looking to drive profitability and enterprise value.

When I say enterprise value, I'm referring to the worth of the business you're building and your future exit strategy: how to maximize everything you've created.

The key to profitability for most businesses is to focus and be incredibly clear on the business you're in and the business you're not. More than ever, FOMO (fear of missing out) plagues our global society. What we see and hear in social media feeds, in the media, and elsewhere is what everyone else has and what we supposedly lack. Whether it's a material possession or an achievement, the message is that you're not good enough, and you're missing out on what's deservedly yours. More, more, more!

The tactics used to sway you from your path have been the same for centuries:

- The bandwagon (now often called social proof)
- Immediate urgency ("Offer expires soon!" or "Someone else will get it and you won't!")

We are emotional beings, and many of our greatest fears lie in the risk of looking stupid. Who hasn't had that dream of showing up in a social setting without clothing?

The secret to long-lasting success in this journey? You *must* do less and do less better.

Every business I've worked with reaches a turning point where there's a recognition: To grow bigger, it must get smaller. This could mean narrowing focus on product offerings, human capital, or infrastructure. Since every business is unique, you have to determine what "smaller" looks like for yours.

Now, every business needs to accrete the sand before it can build the sandcastle; I get that. Before you can work on rate, you have to work on volume. Most businesses must focus on volume at the beginning to build a stable base, just to get past next month's payroll, rent, and other expenses.

If you're entering a competitive market, the fastest way to win customers is usually price. Of course, value and high-end services are intentionally scarce and carry a premium. But for a brand-new offering in a traditional market, leading with a price advantage is often the best play. It's a volume-first strategy before you can increase your rates.

We see this all the time. Take the streaming service market, for example. Media giants launch new platforms in an already saturated space. They enter at $6/month, while competitors charge

$17/month. It's tempting enough for a prospective customer to give it a try.

This is price elasticity at work. When a price falls below a consumer's "radar," they become less sensitive to it. Say I walk into a convenience store. One candy bar costs $1; another, $1.25. I barely register that I've paid 25% more. The same goes for streaming. That $6 service will eventually raise its rate to $8. That's a 33% jump, yet it's still just $2.

Now consider this in higher-ticket markets: a 33% increase on a $450,000 house? Paying $600,000 for an identical home suddenly feels outrageous.

So once your business has entered and survived the market, and you're beginning to build a solid, reliable customer base, the entrepreneur must shift gears.

You may be a solo operator: just you and maybe a part-time assistant or specialist. There's beauty in being a solo act. I often see this in professional services like consulting, legal, accounting, or counseling. These fields require specialized education, licensing, or qualifications.

The flexibility and freedom of being a one-person operation are incredibly attractive. But the risk is real.

Other times, the solo business involves specialized equipment, manufacturing, or a trade skill that creates a niche. The flexibility and freedom of being a one-person operation are incredibly attractive. But the risk is real. If something interrupts your ability to work—disability, family obligations, or unexpected issues—the business stops. The work can't be completed, and in that moment, there is no business.

Last year, I spoke with a man who had owned a machine shop for thirty-five years. He'd listed it for sale through a broker but hadn't sold it in over a year. One buyer needed a two-year apprenticeship before he could take over. The other was a car dealer who only wanted the equipment. Sadly, this man had never built a business, only a job. There was no succession plan. No transferable value except for the machinery sitting in the shop.

This is the reality for many solopreneurs: You haven't necessarily built a business; you've created a high-paying job for yourself. There's no business beyond your own capabilities and capacity.

And that might be just fine. But you must ask yourself:

- What am I building?
- Is this just a high-paying job?
- Is this revenue just a piggy bank, or am I making purposeful investments?

At some point, you'll reach a fork in the road: Do I stay on the lifestyle path (solo operator, full flexibility)? Or do I pursue the enterprise path (building a team, managing systems, creating something that can outlive me)?

Both paths have trade-offs. But if you're looking to build a salable asset with a client list, intellectual capital, equipment, real estate, a unique product, or other scalable assets, you must commit to creating an enterprise business.

Before we dive into financial statements and ratios, let me offer a few observations about the realities of success and things to consider for your business and your life in general:

- Wealth is created in concentrated and highly leveraged positions.
- Happiness is achieved when you embrace contentment.

- Achievement is rarely external but almost always internal.
- Impact is measured in the life you make for others.

WEALTH

In my observation of the financial markets, entrepreneurs, success, and wealth are created in concentrated and highly leveraged positions. When starting from zero, one can save their way to wealth, but it takes unusual discipline to get there, recognizing it's not what you earn but what you save that makes the difference. There are few who are able and willing to be patient enough to forgo in order to achieve wealth.

Doesn't everyone love stories of people like the school janitor who saved so much of their income over fifty years of service that they were able to pay for dozens of children's college tuition? The admiration and respect for someone like that are warranted, and I think most of us wish we had more of that kind of mindset and discipline in us!

I work with and coach multi-millionaires every day, and I've read the same info and books you likely have. From my vantage point, I'll say it again: Wealth is created in concentrated and highly leveraged positions. This isn't Vegas or Monte Carlo; most of the wealthy aren't putting it all on red and letting it ride. They are betting on themselves.

The risk they take is financial, yes, but it is also a risk based on a belief in themselves. As we talked briefly about in the opening, many of those who've achieved wealth feel a calling to build their business, and the wealth is a byproduct, not the original intent.

There's likely a glimmer in the background of starting up, a hope and desire that their efforts will be rewarded monetarily, for sure. But it usually starts with a spark of genius, a passion, or a cause. That journey eventually leads to a move through Maslow's hierarchy of needs, and ultimately, self-actualization and wealth are a result of the risk.

My belief is that the entrepreneur reading this chapter has at least nodded their head and perhaps even muttered an "amen." The entrepreneur is a unique animal: their DNA views risk differently. And with that willingness to concentrate their cash, assets, reputation, and efforts comes the long-awaited reward.

HAPPINESS

I've read that toward the end of his life, Steve Jobs said about wealth, "In the end, wealth is just a fact of life to which I am accustomed... All the recognition and wealth I have are meaningless in the face of imminent death."

I don't think he meant to sound flippant about wealth. The reader could interpret this as a sign of his disconnect from the common person and a casual acceptance of wealth as just a fact of life. However, I believe the intent behind his words is this: If we are truly honest in assessing the purpose of our lives, especially when faced with our mortality, then wealth, recognition, and accolades become relatively insignificant.

So, an introspective review of why you're doing what you're doing as an entrepreneur can be both enlightening and a little frightening. Considering the countless hours and energy we pour into our businesses, a careful accounting may reveal a need for change. Recognition is one thing; actual change is another.

The Exit Planning Institute reports that, based on their global research of entrepreneurs, 75% are dissatisfied to varying degrees after selling their businesses. Even if you're fortunate enough to have a salable business, you're still up against the majority trend of post-sale dissatisfaction, even after you've monetized the asset you spent decades building.

Why is that? How can someone who has achieved so much, overcome incredible odds, and realized financial success still feel dissatisfied after the transaction is complete?

Some of the reasons behind this can be uncovered through a proprietary assessment my team and I developed, building on what we learned during our training in the Certified Exit Planning Adviser (CEPA) curriculum. At the end of this chapter, if you're an entrepreneur within 10 years of exiting your business, I invite you to take our Retirement Readiness Predictor assessment. It will help you evaluate how prepared you are for the next chapter and where you might still need to grow.

Now, when I say that happiness is built on embracing contentment, that may sound like it goes against the DNA of a typical entrepreneur. How can someone whose drive and personality push them to never be content now be asked to consider contentment as their only path to happiness?

"Riddle me this, Batman."

Having worked with thousands of people across hundreds of businesses, I'm telling you: It's true. For all the amazing things that a relentless drive and "never settle" mindset can bring, it can also become too much of a good thing. Without balance, this drive spins out of control and produces a less-than-happy human being. It must be counterbalanced with an appreciation for the peace and satisfaction that contentment can bring.

I'm not a trained psychologist, and forgive me if I don't do the profession justice, but the wisest people I've met suggest this is absolutely true. Simple contentment can mean the difference between a life well-lived and enjoyed and a life marked by regret and disappointment.

So, how does an entrepreneur achieve contentment while still maintaining the drive required to move their business and vision forward?

My humble recommendation: gratitude.

Simple contentment can mean the difference between a life well-lived and enjoyed and a life marked by regret and disappointment.

There's a special place in my heart for several entrepreneurs I know who have figured this out. These men and women have learned how to balance their insatiable desire to achieve with the realization that their greatest achievements may have little to do with their businesses. They are grounded in the belief that their purpose, cause, or passion extends far beyond a business itself.

If your passion is powerful enough to fuel your business, it's likely a cause worthy of pursuing beyond your entrepreneurial venture. Gratitude shows up in the quiet, reflective moments, allowing you to recognize and be content with where you are on the journey.

Much like the story of the wolf you feed, I do believe we each have two forces competing for our attention and identity. The one that dominates is simply the one you choose to feed. I don't mean to imply that your passion is evil and contentment is good. The point is simply that you get what you emphasize.

Questions to ask yourself:

- How often am I reflecting on the blessings in my life?
- Am I investing the time necessary to nourish and foster important relationships?
- Do I have a transition method when moving from one role in life to another?
- Am I present in the thing I'm doing?

- How can I bring my best self to the different roles of my life?

Ultimately, happiness is like a fingerprint. I can't create or design it for you, and you can't do it for me. We all must find our own path to happiness.

If this feels like an area of opportunity for you, a good place to start is by reviewing your core values and your calendar. Can you see evidence of your values in the life you lead, based on how you spend your time? What needs to stay the same? What needs to change?

Over a decade ago, a good friend introduced me to the framework of BAL: Be, Act, Live. This has been invaluable in helping me periodically remember who I am, what I believe, and how I envision living my life.

My BAL statement is something I've memorized and engraved on the fleshy tables of my heart:

- **Be** the Man God Intended
- **Act** Boldly and Unseen Forces Will Come to Your Aid
- **Live** the Life You Want Now

Happiness for me is encapsulated in these three simple yet deeply meaningful phrases, reminders of who I strive to be. Reflecting back on our Purpose Principle, the alignment between the ideal and real self, along with gratitude and contentment, can help you in your journey to achieve happiness, alongside the success and wealth that entrepreneurship can bring.

ACHIEVEMENT

As outlined earlier, "Money, Marbles, and Chalk" doesn't encapsulate all the ways people are professionally motivated, but it's a helpful framework for thinking about achievement. This is so critical, I think it bears reviewing further…

- **Money is self-evident.** Achieving a personal net worth, reaching an income goal, or purchasing something you've worked toward: These are all manifested in how money is saved or spent.
- **Marbles represent tangible recognition of one's achievements.** It's something you can display physically or digitally. Think of a race medal, an Oscar, a certification, or a plaque—tokens that mark a moment in time.
- **Chalk symbolizes verbal or public recognition.** It might be your name written in lights. It could be a shoutout in a team newsletter, a slide in a presentation, or public praise from a respected leader. These are words of affirmation that carry real weight.

Ultimately, we all appreciate recognition for our achievements. Some of us are shy, others dislike the spotlight, but every one of us has a preferred way to feel seen and appreciated.

Ironically, these external acknowledgments are not as long-lasting as the internal satisfaction that comes from achieving something meaningful to us. As mentioned in the People Principle, our greatest victories are often won in the "silent chambers of your own soul."

Much like Steve Jobs, I believe that true fulfillment comes in the privacy of our personal victories: the internal demons we've conquered, the habits we've mastered, and the progress we've made in becoming the person we aspire to be. It is in the becoming that true and meaningful achievement is found.

IMPACT

During my time on the African continent, I experienced a connection with nature that is hard to duplicate anywhere else. The connection went beyond the breathtaking sights of safari or flying over the bush; there was a deep sense of meaning in contemplating the vastness and age of the land. Wisdom seems to echo through those wide-open spaces.

We all admire the speed and agility of a cheetah or the superhuman feats of Usain Bolt in his record-setting sprints. Ferrari World in Abu Dhabi has the fastest rollercoaster in the world, and it lives up to its name. The raw power of an IndyCar or Formula One racer flying past is awe-inspiring.

Speed reveals a rare and exhilarating power, but it's fleeting. When applied to our lives, over the hundred or so years we typically have, focusing only on "getting there fast" can cause us to miss or even destroy what's truly important.

Going at a more measured pace and bringing others along with us is what most of us will remember and appreciate in the end. This is the "going together vs. going alone."

In his book *How Will You Measure Your Life?* Clayton Christensen asks readers to contemplate death: As you look back, how did your life stack up? What mattered? How did you maximize your time?

With every moment, we are making a statement on what matters. While it may feel heavy to consider the people we're impacting during a regular workday or mundane meeting, if you care about longevity and depth of legacy, it becomes imperative to think about your impact.

Impact, then, is measured in the life you make for others more than the life you make for yourself.

Even for those of us who never have a family or children, our life's passion gains meaning because it has influenced or shaped another life. As an entrepreneur, just a typical workday is impacting the lives of others, whether it's through the product or service you provide or the livelihood you offer your employees.

Impact should be a part of your business model. It can be the icon, the standard, or the mission that motivates your team.

I know businesses that measure impact through simple but powerful phrases:

- "America Needs What We Do"
- "Serving 10,000 Families from Coast to Coast"

Even Coca-Cola's mission gives a fizzy drink purpose:

- "Refresh the world. Make a difference."

Ultimately, your impact will hold the most meaning when you consider the life you've made for others.

I've seen tears shed by entrepreneurs who've fulfilled their mission and passed the baton to the next generation. Without exception, the most fulfilled business owners are those most proud and gratified by the lives they've touched.

Let's now turn toward the tactical side of the business. How do the best entrepreneurs think about Profit?

Let's begin with what my team and I have found to be the 10 *critical* financial KPIs every entrepreneur should be benchmarking against industry peers and tracking within their team. These indicators help make sound decisions on resources, capital, and strategic investments.

You've likely heard or even said, "What gets measured gets managed." While clichéd, it's still deeply true.

I can't count the number of times I've seen a marginal or slight change in what a leader chooses to measure and how it suddenly drives massive improvement. People need to know what matters. When they do, and when their beliefs, incentives, and teammates align around those same priorities, the entire organization shifts.

I first came across the article "The Neuroscience of Leadership" decades ago. David Rock and Jeffrey Schwartz authored this powerful white paper from 2006 that outlines how real, meaningful, and long-lasting change happens. The case studies showed that the only thing that consistently drives long-term behavioral change is what they called *attention density*: a focused, consistent emphasis on what matters (Rock and Schwartz, 2006).

Yes, the carrot and the stick work in the short term. But lasting change comes from consistency and clarity of purpose.

Reflecting back on our Purpose Principle and the Leadership TRIP, there's a clear connection between positional power and genuine relationships. Leaders who chase quick compliance through authority sacrifice the potential for sustainable behavior change.

Accuracy, for any leader, is about clarity: the link between purpose and the greater good of the organization. Immediate compliance may feel satisfying, like you've checked something off your leadership to-do list. But if it leads to constantly managing someone just to get results, you've landed in the "tolerated" quadrant of the Leadership TRIP.

Attention density creates long-lasting change. There is no shortcut. No fast pass. You must carefully choose your key performance indicators, focus on them regularly, and ensure that everyone can see them. The Entrepreneurial Operating System (EOS) has a great phrase for this: "Followed By All."

You're not building a cult of blind obedience or obliged compliance. You're building a culture where people's actions align with a committed internal desire to achieve the mission. And your culture needs clear foundations, guiding your team with confidence and direction. As the leader, you must define them.

Here are the 10 critical key financial performance indicators:

- **Gross Profit:** Revenue minus your direct costs (your cost of goods sold)
- **EBOC:** Earnings before owner's compensation (profit after expenses, before owner's pay)
- **Operating Profit:** Earnings before interest and taxes (after direct and operating expenses)
- **Revenue per Owner:** Revenue divided by equity owners (productivity per owner)
- **Revenue per Employee:** Revenue divided by employees (workforce productivity)
- **Revenue per Client/Customer:** Revenue divided by clients/customers (value by client)
- **Direct Expense per Client:** Direct costs divided by clients/customers (cost to serve each)
- **Overhead Payroll:** Compensation for non-client-facing staff (fixed personnel burden)
- **Technology Cost:** Expenses for the tech stack to deliver products/services
- **Marketing Cost:** Expenses for advertising, branding, business development, and affinities

Key Performance Indicators (KPIs) - Quick Reference Sheet

KPI	Description
Gross Profit	Revenue minus direct costs; measures efficiency before overhead.
EBOC	Earnings Before Owner's Compensation; profit after expenses but before owner pay .
Operating Profit	Earnings after direct costs and operating expenses, before interests/taxes.
Revenue per Owner	Revenue divided by number of equity owners; reflects productivity per owner.
Revenue per Employee	Revenue divided by employees; measures workforce efficiency.
Revenue per Client/Customer	Revenue divided by active clients/customers; shows avg. value per client.
Direct Expense per Client	Direct service/product costs allocated per client; cost to serve.
Overhead Payroll	Compensation for non-client-facing staff; measures fixed personnel burden.
Technology Cost	Expenses for software, hardware, licenses. IT infrastructure.
Marketing Cost	Expenses for advertising, branding and client acquisition

Figure 10: KPIs Quick Reference Sheet

I've seen too many business owners rely on their accountant, bookkeeper, or CPA to provide feedback on the state of their business. These professionals are critical, and the work they do is essential for managing finances, paying taxes, and keeping the business running smoothly, no doubt about it.

However, if the entrepreneur isn't directing these professionals on what's important to their specific business, they've essentially taken their hand off the wheel. They're hoping the specialist they've hired somehow knows what matters most, despite serving hundreds of other businesses.

I'm sure you can see the issue here: Good decisions are made based on good information.

So, ask yourself:

- Is the information you're using truly relevant to your business?
- Is it too generalized or too vague to be useful?
- Do you have any form of financial discipline in place to determine whether your business is on track?

My coaching team is passionate about using math and science as the foundation for decision-making. Too often, entrepreneurs lean heavily on intuition, gut feelings, or anecdotal feedback from peers whose situations only appear similar. Developing a method for measurement and benchmarking is critical for business owners to genuinely understand whether they're heading in the right direction.

Our team has developed several benchmarks to help entrepreneurs measure their business performance. Benchmarking against industry peers can be incredibly valuable, especially when the data compares you to businesses in a similar revenue band. This lets you assess your performance against both current and aspirational (future) peers and gain insight into whether you're operating above, below, or at par.

Developing a method for measurement and benchmarking is critical for business owners to genuinely understand whether they're heading in the right direction.

That said, being above, below, or at par only means something in the context of your unique business. For example, you might appear to overspend in a certain category relative to peers, but that overspending may be strategic: an intentional investment aligned with your growth stage or future plans.

This is where I must emphasize a key point: Relying on professional advisers requires discernment. You may benefit from limiting the scope of their advice to areas where they hold true expertise, while simultaneously developing your own financial discipline and methodology to reach the right conclusions.

Here's the most important point when it comes to benchmarking: If your data is different from that of your peers by design, there's no problem. You have a strategy, and you're sticking to it.

The problem arises when you're different by happenstance.

Animals, objects, and things are subject to their environment and external stimuli. The better entrepreneur knows they are an agent of action, and that mindset is critical in financial management.

REVENUE PER CLIENT (RPC): A LITMUS TEST

Of the 10 critical financial KPIs, my favorite is Revenue per Customer/Client (RPC). It's a fundamental litmus test for your business, directly tied to your:

- Pricing strategy
- Ideal client profile
- Overhead
- Client or customer segmentation

By leveraging this single data point, you can gain sharp insight into performance, especially if you have peer data on customer investment levels from firms of similar scope and scale.

Like a well-woven tapestry, this financial metric is interconnected with multiple elements. Pull one thread—pricing, ideal client, overhead, or client segments—and you affect the others.

Let's start with client segments and work backward.

Client Segmentation: Foundation of RPC

Take a specialty service business with:

- Long-term client relationships
- A recurring fee model
- Retention rates in the 90%+ range

Businesses like these typically show consistent RPC over time. That historical consistency makes the metric reliable and valuable.

At this early stage, RPC is viewed as a broad figure, regardless of client segments or product lines. The next step is to identify concentrations within those segments and lines. Where are you generating value, and where are you not?

In retail wealth management, we recommend segmenting clients by revenue into three groups:

- Top 20% (highest revenue)
- Next 80% (split as needed into additional segments)

If your business size allows, a four-tiered system can work well:

- 20% in the top tier
- 30% in the next two tiers
- 20% in the bottom tier

Our findings, almost without exception, show that half of a wealth management business's clients generates 90% or more of total revenue, while the other half generates less than 10%.

There are many reasons for this "haves and have-nots" scenario. You might relate to this. Like many business owners, growth for growth's sake may have quietly crept in. To build the castle, you must accrete the sand. I get that. But without a strategic vision defining your ideal client, the business begins to accept any client who can fog a spoon.

RPC AND COST: THE REAL PICTURE

When we talk about Revenue per Client (RPC), the expense side of the equation quickly follows. So, while it's my favorite metric, RPC must be viewed alongside your P&L for proper context.

Before even pulling industry benchmarks, calculate a simple "carrying cost" or rough breakeven: Take your total business costs (the "L" side of the P&L) and divide by client headcount. Now, work with RPC and carrying cost together to uncover the real issue. Remember: *"For every thousand hacking at the leaves, one is hacking at the root."*

In our wealth management example, the bottom half of clients is likely creating dysfunction. Even worse, the top half may be subsidizing the experience of those lower-revenue clients. These less-than-ideal customers are also getting more than their fair share of your team's time and resources. Relatively speaking, the hour they take of your systems, resources, or services is costing you more than the hour that an ideal customer takes.

Would you be comfortable telling your most valuable client that their fees are subsidizing thirty others? Probably not.

But let's be fair: just because a client is below breakeven doesn't mean they lack value. There's nuance here:

- Historical pricing may be outdated.
- They may be family or close connections to high-value clients.
- There may be long-term potential or strategic value.

So don't lump all low-revenue clients into one bucket. Investigate further:

- Are they friends or family?
- A future opportunity?
- Do they provide value unique to your business?

Measurement matters. RPC and carrying cost together provide a "true north" to guide decisions.

Many businesses lose profits by serving the wrong customers. Clients below breakeven often take as much time and attention as your most profitable ones (or even more). That's a problem. And usually, it stems from unclear client profiles or that old nemesis: growth for growth's sake.

REVENUE PER EMPLOYEE (RPE): EFFICIENCY MEETS ALIGNMENT

Another favorite KPI of mine is Revenue per Employee (RPE). Yes, we're still focused on topline revenue, but for good reason: Revenue is the great equalizer.

You can track market share, assets per client, loyalty, reviews, click-throughs, and site visits—the list goes on. But when you have clarity around your revenue drivers, broken down by key elements of your business, you're working with the kind of information that leads to smart, aligned action.

RPE measures your team's effectiveness: their efficiency and efficacy per dollar generated.

It's also a widely used metric across industries, which makes it valuable for benchmarking. The best teams I coach use this number as a driver in their business planning. It keeps operations and finance aligned.

There's real value in the productive tension between operations' desire for more human capital and finance's mandate to manage EBITDA. RPE can serve as the middle ground, the shared metric that keeps both sides honest.

My daughter was recently promoted to district leader at a local movie theater chain. In her new role, she gained deeper insight into how the business makes money. One of her training takeaways was that the theater had a target of 11% overhead allocated to staff costs on the floor and behind the tills serving customers.

Her boss proudly shared that the business had been operating at 9% for months, well below the target. Sounds great, right? But my daughter had been working multiple roles during shifts, covering kitchen, concessions, and tills, while training new staff and performing her own duties.

You might say, "She's a district leader. That's what she signed up for." And you'd be right. But the target exists for a reason. Running below it might improve the financials, but it also increases turnover and stretches staff too thin. Ultimately, she left the job.

Remember our discussion on price elasticity? The 2% delta, on the surface, may not appear to be significant. However, if we follow the math (percent gain divided by target = 2/11), that is an 18% gain in cost efficiency that came at a steep price. The effective business owner recognizes that "beating the metric" may not always be in the company's long-term best interest.

Are you making short-term bets that feel good at the moment but impede your long-term strategy?

In his research on hundreds of companies, author Jim Collins identified the difference between good and great companies: Discipline.

The root of discipline? Discipleship.

Religious overtones aside, this is important. Disciples follow a set of beliefs and values that shape their behavior and guide their commitment. Likewise, the better entrepreneur is grounded in a purpose, cause, or passion that shapes their company and builds systems that reflect those values. Having the discipline to hold the vision through inevitable market shifts and tempting opportunities is what separates good from great. The most powerful cultures I've seen talk about "the mission" and how important it is to put one's own individual or departmental needs aside in pursuit of the greater good of that mission.

Reacting to every wind and shiny new object breaks clarity, message, and momentum. The willingness to sacrifice short-term wins for long-term success reflects leadership maturity. Your chosen KPIs should guide your firm in the direction you intend to go, not just where you are today. What is mission-critical? I think of the true story as reenacted in the movie *Apollo 13*. The number of things that went wrong on that particular mission seems almost unreal. Truth is truly stranger than fiction. When the specialists on the ground finally determined that power was the key to success or failure, they were able to focus their attention and what they measured for success on the things that were only mission-critical. The mission had always been to preserve the sanctity of human life in the pursuit of further space exploration. When the commander boldly stated, "I believe this will be our finest moment..." he was referring to the team's ability to face incredible odds and bring the astronauts home. If you're to be the best entrepreneurial leader you can be, you must ask yourself, *What is the mission, and what is mission-critical?*

Identifying what's important is one of the most critical decisions a business owner can make.

You don't need thirty KPIs. Ten or fewer is my recommendation. Too many, and your team gets lost in the weeds. Too few, and you risk tunnel vision, leading to imbalance and dysfunction. KPIs must represent what truly matters to your business. And identifying what's important is one of the most critical decisions a business owner can make.

The military uses an After Action Report (AAR) process: review the mission, what was done, what worked, and what didn't. This structured feedback loop helps improve future performance. Most businesses don't do this. If you don't have an AAR process, start one. Your financial discipline, KPI selection, trend tracking, and data-based decisions will all improve when you pause, reflect, and learn from your results.

Let's circle back to RPE. Yes, you can hit your RPE goal by:

- Increasing productivity per team member, or
- Simply reducing headcount.

But metrics alone don't tell the whole story. Without leadership clarity and alignment with purpose, a business can lose its soul, even if the numbers look great. That's why metrics must always be guided by mission.

The key takeaway from this Profit Principle is simple: Identify the metrics and indicators that make the most sense for your business and your team. Keep the list manageable. Choose them wisely. Use them consistently. And most importantly, align them with the true direction of your business, not just what's easy to measure. See the QR code at the beginning or end of the book that leads you to more resources as you contemplate your Profitability.

Now, on to our final principle: Potential.

PRINCIPLE 5: POTENTIAL

In my team's experience coaching hundreds of businesses and thousands of business owners, the focus in your business typically falls somewhere along a continuum of three stages. You are either:

1. Building a better team,
2. Building a better business, or
3. Seeking better freedom from operating the business.

Some reflection here might be in order as you consider: *What am I working on in my business?*

You've likely said, "Working *on* the business vs. working *in* the business." This reflection is all about unlocking the potential within your business.

If you're in the stage of building a better team, the focus is on structure first, people second. The design of your organization is just as important as the people you currently have, or plan to have, on the team.

The design of your organization is just as important as the people you currently have,

The "building a better business" stage focuses on "professionalizing" your enterprise across key areas such as finance, operations, strategic planning, and exit planning. It's about developing greater intentionality in how you manage and grow the business.

The freedom stage is where the founder or tenured successor is working to step out of being the focal point of the business. Ownership may or may not change hands, but this stage certainly requires the owner to begin transferring tribal knowledge, experience, and expertise to the next generation of doers within the business.

Working on any of these stages allows the better entrepreneur to unlock the business's true potential at that given stage. While it may seem like the three stages of potential should occur sequentially (and in many cases, they do), the reality is that disruptions, mergers, consolidations, or acquisitions can impact the natural progression.

Let's work through each of these three stages individually and identify the potential that's either sitting dormant or actively being unlocked, depending on whether the leader is truly working on the business (or not).

So, what about building a better team? What is the critical nature of the potential in this stage, and how do you know you're currently in it?

While this may not have aged well for those with more refined humor, years ago, Jeff Foxworthy had a famous comedy act called "You might be a redneck if…" In the spirit of self-identifying your current stage, here are some telltale signs you're in the Building a Better Team stage:

- You have a great team with raw talent, but you receive consistent feedback that there's not enough clarity on roles, career paths, or how people can gain ownership in your firm.
- Your leadership team is just you or a very small group of people who are overwhelmed with "people issues."
- You are struggling with new client or customer acquisition. (Remember the "5 Signs It's Time to Hire or Fire," from the People Principle?)
- There is no clear successor for a leadership seat that is either already overdue to be filled or will soon need to be.
- You have multiple team members who are a great fit for your culture but are not in the right roles.
- Worse yet, you have more than one team member who is clearly not a fit, but you're holding onto them due to fear of backlash, a capacity gap that their departure would create, or simply because of their tenure on the team.
- The scale of your business is such that losing even one team member creates a significant burden, reducing overall productivity or hampering your ability to deliver on business development or client acquisition goals.

Let's now review some scenarios that may indicate you're working on Building the Better Business:

- You are struggling to "see" the financials of your business regularly and consistently. You need a structure and discipline in financial management, a tight process of monthly budgets, P&L data, and margins/ratios that guide the leadership team on the financial health of the company.

- Your leadership team may have titles, but the function each plays is unclear. People on the team are not certain who their "boss" is, and you find cultural issues and breakdowns related to leadership and the members of the team they are meant to lead.
- You've fallen prey to what I call the **Three C's of Culture Systems: Career Paths, Compensation, and Cultivation.** These three silent killers quietly erode your firm's culture from the inside out. When **career paths** are undefined, **compensation** feels ambiguous or like a mysterious black box, and **cultivation**—the development and training of your people—is haphazard or inconsistent, the result is a culture built on confusion rather than clarity. Promotions start to feel arbitrary, based on gut feelings, moods, or likability rather than a structured plan. There's no documented approach to career progression, compensation becomes subjective and inconsistent, and skill development depends more on individual grit than on intentional leadership. Without clear definitions in these three areas, your best people eventually disengage or leave, and the culture you've worked so hard to build begins to crumble.
- The next generation of leaders and/or owners has not been identified. The business is stagnant because most things have to filter through you. There's either an unspoken question in your top talent about their place on the succession map, or it comes up often and creates conflict between you and the people on the team you rely on.

- People appear not to be clear on what a successful day looks like. Everyone is accountable, which really means that no one is, and it is hard to discover how daily actions turn into daily results.
- Performance reviews either don't happen at all or, when they do, take the form of a shallow box-checking discussion. Compensation and performance are not clearly linked, and bonuses are discretionary without metrics to determine merit.
- The strategic vision is either locked up in your head as the entrepreneur and not shared by all, or you have it documented and shared, but the team consistently misses goals, deadlines, or milestones, leading to a lack of belief or interest in the firm's future.

Lastly, let's look at common characteristics of a business that needs to work on Building Better Freedom:

- **You are the bottleneck:** The business is so dependent upon you that the thought of a vacation, a long weekend, or a sabbatical would spell impending disaster for the company or create such a wave of work on your return that it's simply not worth it!
- **The business has no documented succession plan:** If you go down, not only do the business's operations suffer, but the actual enterprise value tanks as well. You are likely a significant majority or 100% owner and don't have a way to monetize or de-risk your wealth from the value of the business.
- **Your business runs you; you don't run the business:** Your personal calendar, personal relationships, and

well-being are all tied to the firm's success. As the business goes, so goes you.

- **You've neglected health, personal hobbies or ambitions, and personal relationships for the sake of the business:** You're ready to change it, but you don't know where to begin.
- **When you do take time away from the business, you are still conducting business:** You don't have confidence in the members of your team to carry on or make decisions without your involvement. You check email during a game, movie, or idle time on the beach; respond to texts at dinner; or answer calls as you walk from one experience to another.
- **You're not present in what you're supposed to be doing:** There is no compartmentalization of your life or relationships. You are sacrificing the things that truly matter for the things that feel truly urgent.
- **There's no structure to your next chapter:** As you gain more freedom from the operations and day-to-day of the business, you've not clearly articulated what you're going to do. You're clear on what you're moving from, but the next time and location are not defined.

There are likely other features that can further explain what each of these stages or steps along the business-building journey looks and feels like, but these seven characteristics for each phase are a great starter list to orient you to where you are in the journey.

Now that we've calibrated our GPS, let's dive into how you can unlock the pent-up potential in each of these areas of your business:

- Building a Better Team
- Building a Better Business
- Building Better Freedom

This is the stage where the proverb mentioned earlier really comes into play: "If you want to go fast, go alone. If you want to go far, go together."

When the entrepreneur first starts their business, they are rewarded for behavior that is actually detrimental and counter-productive to their business in its mature state. "Eat what you kill" is a common way people describe the motivation and attitude it takes to persevere through those first several years of a start-up.

The second and third generations of the business never truly understand the pains, stresses, and sacrifices made by the founder to start and keep the business alive long enough to go beyond the statistics. We've all heard the facts. The Bureau of Labor Statistics painfully reports that 20% of businesses fail in their first year, 50% are gone within five years, and fully 65% of businesses have closed by the ten-year mark. Wrapped inside these cold, hard figures is all the dedication, grit, sacrifice, struggle, and a little divine intervention it takes.

The founder, in these early stages, benefits from a lone-wolf mindset. Leadership is lonely, but never as lonely as in those first years. You might have a significant headcount, depending on your business and industry, but the saying "It's lonely at the top" still applies. Even with a large team in place at start-up, the combination of leverage and concentrated ownership can create a silo that feels quite unnerving.

Even after passing through the stages of building a team and then building a business, most entrepreneurs never fully address the freedom components: diversified ownership, succession planning, and making themselves replaceable. There's a real hit of dopamine and fuel for the ego when the business you started, nurtured, and built depends on your unique talents and abilities.

Who doesn't want to be loved, appreciated, and depended upon?

It's been said that human connection is the greatest determinant of mental health and the avoidance of depression (for those without chronic or external factors). There's no greater connection than being needed and appreciated for who you are and what you do. Many entrepreneurs gain that fulfillment almost exclusively through the businesses they've built. The business becomes their identity, and when or if they are separated from it, the void can be significant.

Freedom can become a prison if it's not carefully considered, planned for, and implemented over time.

To achieve Better Freedom, think of the three legs of the stool:

- The business and its ability to function properly without you
- The financial requirements when you are no longer a major contributor to business growth
- The personal fulfillment and meaning that define a life well-lived

Your plan for these three legs of the Better Freedom Plan (BFP) should begin years in advance of when you intend to step back from day-to-day operations.

Sadly, due to poor planning, the Exit Planning Institute found that 75% of business owners are dissatisfied or greatly dissatisfied just twelve months after exiting their business (Exit Planning Institute, 2013). What a tragedy: to have built something for decades only to feel disappointment in the ultimate outcome.

Declaring freedom doesn't always require selling your business, but it does require a shift in how you spend your time and who you spend it with. My coaching team and I work extensively in this space, and the emotions involved are significant. Decades of anchored behavior must be carefully unpacked to arrive at the right solution. There's no one-size-fits-all answer, but there are core elements within each of the three legs of the Freedom stool that deserve exploration.

THE BUSINESS SOLUTION

There are four intangibles that influence the value of your business. In my work as a Certified Exit Planning Adviser (CEPA), I've found that while most business valuations are built on the health of financial metrics (like EBITDA, profit margins, inventory, depreciable assets, and cash on hand), these intangible benefits of capital can meaningfully enhance valuation.

When business owners begin to understand these four characteristics, they realize how focusing on them can increase their company's value by 15% or more. For many, that's a life-changing difference.

The first intangible is human capital. On a spectrum of strength, the most effective business leaders have a documented process and discipline for recruiting, motivating, and training their teams, and for developing those teams as the organization grows.

The next intangible is customer capital. The best of the best can demonstrate the strength of their customer or client relationships through tenure, wallet share, and depth of commitment, often reinforced by long-term contractual obligations. These customers view your business as an integral part of their success and transformation.

The third intangible capital is structural. This has everything to do with "what gets measured gets managed." Have you documented the 20% of your processes that drive 80% of the results? The core company processes need not only to be documented, but equally important is their transferability to the rest of the team. For too many entrepreneurs, they have a wealth of tribal knowledge that is locked up in the brain of the founder. This creates not only a bottleneck but also a significant risk. Structural capital also includes effective use and management of equipment, technology, and facilities. Does your business have a strategy to optimize the financial and capital structure, and is it transferable to the next owners?

Our final intangible capital is social. In our ever-evolving economy and society, social capital has two faces, internal and external. Is the company culture transferable to the next owner? Does the firm's influence in the community and on social media have the strength to last beyond the founder?

To make the most of your four forms of intangible capital, your company must have a game plan to assess, prioritize, and implement a plan for strengthening each of these areas.

If you're simply not sure where to start in the intangible capital space, ask yourself the following questions:

Assess:

- Do I have a way to measure my effectiveness in each of the four intangibles?
- Is this important enough to the company to take action?
- Do I know if I'm making progress?

Prioritize:

- Is there clarity about any intangible issue and how this can impact the company?
- Do the team's actions and behaviors related to this intangible indicate its priority for me as the owner?
- As the owner, have I invested in this intangible to move the needle?

Implement:

- Is the plan around the intangible actionable, measurable, and meaningful?
- Is the design built for scale?
- Is someone accountable for the project? (Remember, when everyone's responsible, no one is.)

THE FINANCIAL SOLUTION

As the transition from founder to the next generation or an outside buyer unfolds, the ability to rewind a decade earlier is what almost every entrepreneur wishes for. Although hindsight is 20/20, the better entrepreneur recognizes the need to begin working through how to handle the financial implications of what more freedom for themselves actually means.

As outlined in The Business Solution, there are four intangible forms of capital that influence the value of a business. For the financial solution to be maximized, moving your valuation up and to the right in the value quadrants, it must be built on the bedrock of a strong EBITDA. Most business sales, whether internal or external, are calculated based on the firm's earnings performance.

We recommend taking your analysis further by reviewing your P&L through an additional lens, commonly referred to as a recast P&L. This approach offers a more accurate picture of the business by incorporating items such as

- EBOC (Earnings Before Owner's Compensation)
- Special items the owner may take as "creative" income (e.g., a spouse listed as an employee but not actively involved)
- Deductions or expenses that would disappear once the founder exits

This recast provides a clearer view of what the buyer is actually purchasing and a more refined understanding of the business's true valuation.

A well-prepared entrepreneur will also have established a mechanism for others to share in the financial risk, gradually removing the burden of 100% ownership over time.

If you think of ownership in your business as a ladder leaning against the wall of your organization, that ladder has three primary rungs to help someone move from non-ownership to full partnership:

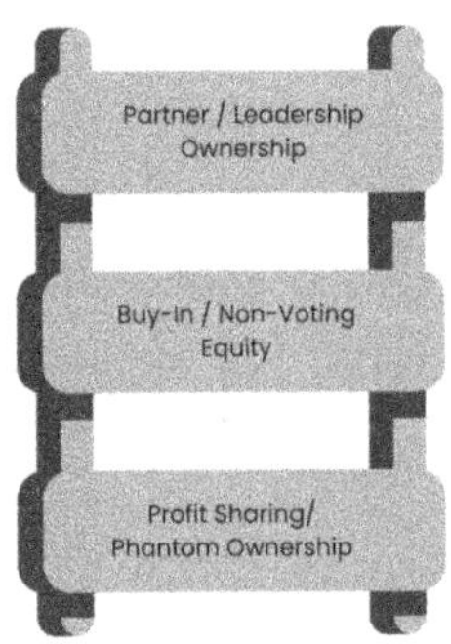

First Rung: Mindset & Habits

This stage is about fostering the mindset and habits needed for future partners to appreciate the value of owning a piece of the business.

It's been said, "No one washes a rental car." I've rented hundreds of cars in my lifetime and have yet to wash one, and I only fill it up when required (lol).

The goal is to get people onto the ladder first, then help them move up the ladder over time. This can be facilitated through phantom equity or profit-sharing plans, which offer flexibility while allowing the founder to retain full control and equity. These plans can also act as a "down payment" or discount toward future, actual equity ownership.

Second Rung: True Buy-In

This is my personal belief, but if someone is going to be an owner, they should go through the rite of passage of securing financing, servicing debt, and understanding the true value of equity.

This rung doesn't come with voting or veto power, nor does it require them to be on the leadership team. However, they do need to pay for their ownership. They'll receive the same rights as other shareholders at their level, including profit distributions and capital gains. With an annual valuation, you can establish a unit or share price that fluctuates with business performance.

Third Rung: Partnership

At this level, the equity owner likely holds 10% or more of the business. They now gain voting rights (even if not decisive) and greater responsibilities.

Each rung serves both as a lesson and a behavioral development step. Even junior partners may be called upon to contribute capital when profits are thin, cover payroll during tough times, and invest in strategic growth initiatives. Most partners at this stage also take on leadership roles within departments, divisions, or C-suite functions.

The point here is simple: There should be an organized approach to developing your successors and the next generation of owners over time.

I've seen too many businesses hand off ownership instantly to a second or third generation, and boy, do they have a lot to learn. You simply cannot expect anyone to absorb thirty to fifty years of experience overnight. It's unrealistic, and no one is naturally up to the task.

It's never too early to start working through an organized transfer of financial risk and ownership burden from one to several. A few final thoughts:

- One hundred percent ownership of a business that's valued at zero is zero. While extreme, it proves the point: Your business is worth significantly more if it has a path to ownership and a tenured leadership team in place. In my experience, such businesses are worth upward of 15% more. (Remember the story of the gentleman trying to sell his business where he was the only employee? Ultimately, it was only worth the equipment.)

- If your entire net worth is tied up in your business, you're playing Russian roulette with your future if you haven't planned the financial piece. When you are both the key operator and sole owner, if you go down, the business goes down. Like a house of cards, your financial security collapses. In this case, you are the business, and the business is you.

THE PERSONAL FULFILLMENT SOLUTION

Some 76% of business owners who've sold their business are dissatisfied with the sale.

In peeling back the layers of this data, it's illuminating to find that most of the dissatisfaction comes from factors other than the financials of the transaction.

One would think: *If a seller gets the price they want, or close to it, shouldn't they be happy?* Well, the short answer is no. The dissatisfaction is often linked to one or more of the following retirement satisfaction predictors:

- **Perspective:** The owner's clarity of mind regarding post-business life and their emotional grounding in the changes
- **Finances:** The nature and stability of financial resources not tied to the business
- **Expectations:** The owner's understanding of and alignment with what they anticipated life would be like after the sale
- **Community:** The depth and quality of the owner's connection to the community they expected to engage with

- **Health:** The owner's physical and mental preparedness to enjoy life at a high quality
- **Involvement:** The degree to which the owner has experience with or a sense of contribution in life outside of the business

My team and I leverage an online portal to guide owners through a process that helps them explore their understanding and readiness for post-business life. While "retirement" is the commonly used term, the definition varies dramatically from person to person.

To be fair, many business owners experience a gradual journey when unwinding from the business. Some never leave and instead become minority owners. It can be disorienting to go from having everyone rely on you to only a few. As you reduce your role in the business, you need a plan to manage your personal experience across each of these predictors.

We've found that our proprietary Owner Readiness tool makes a significant difference in helping an owner understand where to begin when transitioning the business to the next owner(s). If you're within ten years of a potential wind-down or exit, leverage the QR code at the beginning or end of this book to see what your predictor score reveals about your readiness for life *on the other side.*

Why start this process up to 10 years before an event?

As you've likely experienced, life moves quickly, and most business owners are simply not adept at focusing on their personal situation outside of work. They are almost always consumed with building a better team or building a better business.

Freedom often becomes a "nice-to-have" that's put off with the mindset, "I'll get there when I get there."

By taking a personal inventory of your strengths and weaknesses related to these predictors, you can proactively put plans in place to prepare for the inevitable.

With any decision, you typically have four options:

- **Do it:** Take immediate action and invest your time and energy to complete the task.
- **Delegate it:** Still take action, but assign the responsibility to someone else, leveraging their time and hourly rate.
- **Drop it:** Decide it's not important, and intentionally remove it, saving time, energy, and resources.
- **Delay it:** If you're like most peers, this is likely what you've done when it comes to planning for the next chapter of your life.

Delaying can work for a time, but time will continue to pass. And when a task returns, it may do so with more urgency and less time to course-correct.

Your future self will thank your present self for proactively preparing for the inevitable.

If you can't find the motivation to do this for yourself, then consider the people around you, the ones you love and care about.

Just like death or disability can be catastrophic to the value of your business, a lack of clarity and preparedness can feel catastrophic to your family and friends.

If you enter the next chapter of your life unprepared, there's a strong chance that your best self will not show up.

While we've reviewed the predictors, some of the considerations in your readiness are more tangible than the items defined above. Here is a more compelling list of actions and items you need to have in place to be fully confident in your personal preparedness.

- **A written personal plan:** Consider your interests outside of the business: hobbies, passions, or new skills to develop.
- **A personal financial plan:** Usually developed by a professional like a CFP® or financial planner, this provides a view of the owner's current financial situation and future projections based on financial assumptions.
- **A personal estate and tax plan:** Sometimes included as part of the personal financial plan, this outlines the impacts on the estate and tax liability in the case of estate settlement and ongoing taxes due.
- **Personal knowledge of proceeds:** A knowledge check on how any proceeds would be paid out and an estimate of the net proceeds.
- **Post-business income needs:** Another knowledge check—What is your awareness of current spending versus post-business income requirements?
- **Dependency on income from the business:** How much of your current income is dependent upon the business?
- **Knowledge of the transition process:** How well do you understand the requirements and non-negotiables of a quality transition?
- **Advisory team:** The extent to which you've put professionals in place to assist with the transition (CPA, CFP®, Exit Planning Adviser, Attorney, etc.).

- **Defined contingency plan:** A plan for the certainty of uncertainty: disability, death, divorce, or other disruptors, with suitable funding for each.
- **Knowledge of ideal structure:** An understanding of the pros and cons of different exit options and potential deal structures.
- **Family awareness:** The level of family awareness and engagement in the business separation process and the level of involvement you want them to have through discussions and formalized meetings.

We're talking about potential in this chapter. As you look at the list of eleven items above, think of the potential impact of not having clarity and strength in each of these areas—the potential for catastrophe, disappointment, and frustration. On the flip side, when you have strength and clarity in each of these areas, your chance for success, fulfillment, and the ultimate impact you're hoping for, for yourself and those around you, increases significantly. Potential can be quantified and controlled when you educate yourself and put the readiness pieces in place.

As an entrepreneur, it's imperative to become an expert in all of these things. You cannot "kick the can down the road." Remember, you have 4 "D"s with any task or decision: Do it, Delegate it, Drop it, or Delay it. My plea with you is that, in this instance, you "Do it." You don't want to delay further, and you certainly can't drop it. For the betterment of your situation, your team, your customers/clients, and your loved ones, identifying the impact that taking care of your next chapter will have is incredible.

When considering items that are of greatest importance, understanding and managing risk is your greatest asset. Do you really understand the risk you're taking by not having these questions answered? Do you realize the exponential leverage you have when you've harnessed this risk and leveraged it to your advantage? How much more can your business be worth if you have a plan in place?

So, what are the next steps? You're welcome to engage my team in a formalized assessment of how prepared and educated you are in the process. You likely can eyeball your current situation by giving yourself a score for each item on the list and then prioritizing based on the urgency of what you need to work on. Ultimately, you must do something. Make the time, be deliberate, and make the plan. Like with other things that *must* get done, there are five steps to goal achievement: have a goal, have a plan, work the plan, control direction, and throw off discouragement.

Doug Lennick, founder of Think2Perform, offers these five simple steps as part of his "What Do You Want For Yourself?" plan (WDYWFY). When you've aligned values and behaviors as discussed in the alignment model during our Purpose Principle chapter, you will be willing to go through any *how* to achieve your *why*. You must simply determine: Is the pain of the negative consequences of an unplanned or unorganized transition from your business greater or less than the pain of taking the time, investing the resources, and applying the necessary energy to solve the outstanding issues/weaknesses in your current transition plan?

As we wrap up our chapter on potential, I'd like to work through the merger and acquisition opportunities that may be on your horizon. If you are in a maturing industry, you may see a rapid increase in consolidations. If you are seeking potential and opportunity for your firm to capture market share, customers/clients, or talent, acquisition or merger/consolidation may be a great business to be in. I say business for the fact that consistent growth in this manner requires a whole strategic plan with its own collateral, marketing, and human capital to make it happen.

If you're looking at a single acquisition or consolidation, you can get away with "muscling" your way through the minutiae of a single transaction. But if you see the potential in making this something new that you do, you will want to be deliberate and organized in your approach.

The first place to begin is to determine what kind of acquirer you plan to be. In my experience, you have three options for approaching the acquisition space: as a consolidator, integrator, or reseller.

- As a consolidator, you are acquiring businesses that you intend to bring under your umbrella, but they may continue under their existing brand or, at a minimum, continue to have a different operating system and cadence—an affiliation only, with no cultural impacts.
- As an integrator, you are looking to bring in these acquisitions to conform to and align with your operating system and cadence for a more fundamental cultural integration.
- When you are a reseller, you look for acquisitions with partial components that you need or want, and you plan to package up what doesn't fit and resell it to another buyer.

I caution beginners in this journey not to describe themselves as hybrids or say they're open to all three. The more focused your scope when identifying opportunities, the more effective you will be at finding a good acquisition. Too many entrepreneurs I know have been enticed by possibilities and opportunities that fell outside their core competencies or the right fit for their business. They either spend way too much time distracted from their core business or, even worse, make an acquisition that is not a good fit and bring their entire team into a swirling mess of misfits, confusion, and disruption.

If you're not able to narrow focus and clarify what you want, I would recommend steering clear of the acquisition world. It can chew you up and spit you out without batting an eye.

Now, once you've identified what kind of acquirer you want to be, you can use the 5Ps to your advantage. There's an order of importance for how to leverage them in acquisitions vs. mergers (we'll discuss that next). When looking at acquisitions, the order of operations for vetting whether the acquisition is the right fit depends on your chosen acquisition lane.

There's wisdom in a co-mingling of the consolidator and integrator strategies if they are meant to be on a continuum. If you identify an opportunity that is better suited as a consolidation target, with the potential to be fully integrated into the core business over a series of years, that can make a lot of sense. You have to know yourself (your mixture of IQ, EQ, and CQ) and your leadership team's ability to flex through these changes. I've worked with entrepreneurs and their teams who've demonstrated this ability very well. It only works one way—from consolidator to integrator—but it can be a great model that allows the acquiree to gain comfort and confidence in becoming an integrated part of the overall business.

That having been said, for the purposes of how to use the 5Ps in your process, we will assume three distinct strategies. The following chart shows what you should be looking at as a consolidator, integrator, and reseller:

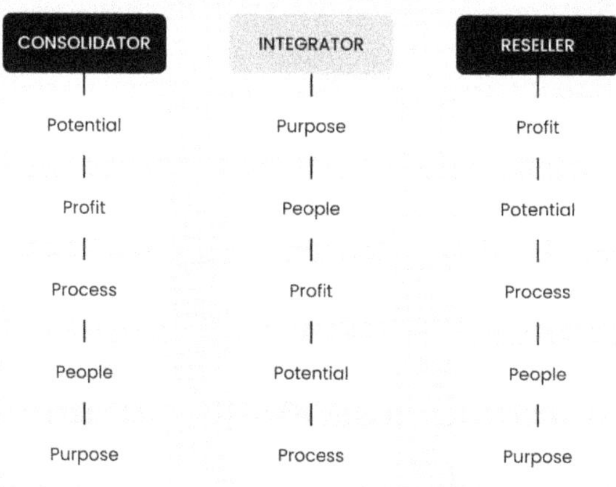

Figure 11: Prioritizing The 5Ps Characteristics

For all acquisitions (and mergers, for that matter), your mindset should be 1 + 1 = 11. We are talking about quantum growth. Of course, I've worked with business owners who've done very well with micro-acquisitions; their strategy is bite-sized chunks that easily fold into their existing business, allowing them to manage capacity and infusions in very surgical steps. This is a great way for those with limited capital or a very low appetite for risk to grow and scale at a pace unachievable through organic growth alone. However, for those who are taking larger swings at bat, the 5Ps can be an incredibly powerful tool to keep the business owner focused on what's important, what needs to be vetted, and the priority, depending on your strategy.

To demonstrate, the consolidator should be thinking about potential. Does this affiliate drive margins in a way that is meaningful? Does the business in question have a strong propensity to grow on its own? The potential for margin expansion while taking on minimal risk is what we're referring to. In many cases, the consolidator will take a minority ownership stake in the affiliate's business to offer marginal influence with the board of the acquiree or with the business owner themselves. Profit is a fast follower in order of importance. As I mentioned, if the acquiree is marginally profitable or doesn't have great cash flow, they can quickly become a drag on margins, as the affiliate model usually lends itself to thinner margins. The process, people, and purpose elements are relevant but less important, since the affiliate will, many times, retain their brand and operating system as currently constituted. So, the acquirer need not "meddle" in these areas at this stage of acquisition.

The integrator needs to focus most on purpose. You might say to yourself, "Well, if the profit isn't there, I can't make the deal work," and you'd be correct. However, as we look at the list of priorities, I am not suggesting that you throw any of the 5Ps out the window due to the order of importance. What I am saying is that your primary focus here is on purpose. Is there alignment of values, cultural norms, and attitudes that lead to this acquisition, enhancing and supporting your core business's culture, or not? If not, it doesn't matter how profitable the business is; you are destined to end up in divorce.

I am currently working with a client who's in the beginning stages of a very messy divorce with her partner. As part of this integration, the client received some professional advice that caused more damage than good. The agreements were not all in place and were poorly written in the first place. I just started working with this entrepreneur, and perhaps I'm being too flippant about the history of the relationship, but there doesn't appear to have been enough due diligence spent on culture, personality, personal and professional behavior, and values. Now we are dealing with a hostile and tenuous relationship. It is very clear that values and belief systems are not aligned and never really were. Integration is risky business if the purpose is not aligned. You create a hostage situation with the acquired, and the acquirer shouldn't be expected to kowtow to the acquiree's culture.

A word to the wise: Start with purpose and be a fast follower of people before you get too enamored with profit. In many of these acquisitions, what you're truly buying is the talent. Purpose and people (the talent) are the lifeblood of your culture, and culture must be nurtured and protected at all costs to achieve greatness.

The reseller needs to be less concerned here with purpose and people. As a matter of fact, they may not have any relevance to this strategy. The reseller is focused on the transactional nature of the acquisition and the chance to capture or capitalize on the profit, potential, and margin of the business being acquired. Unless there is a key member of the team that is critical to making the acquisition work, the reseller should spend their time evaluating the profit, potential, and process of the business. They can live with negative cultural impacts in the acquisition and focus on the portion of the acquisition that is most relevant to their objectives.

The way to win in the reseller strategy is speed: getting the portion of the business they need and reselling the portion they don't. The sooner they can manage through the acquisition and resale, the sooner they can take advantage of the capital capture in the additional sale. This is a turnover play, kind of like flipping houses, but in this case, the buyer isn't interested in fixing it up; they just need the part that's working and tangential to their core business while getting rid of the part that isn't relevant.

For mergers, the 5Ps are just as valuable. Like the integrator above, a merger is a coming together of cultures, people, beliefs, and processes. I recommend that the integrator's path through the 5Ps be similar, if not identical. If you don't have a marriage of purpose and people, you don't have a marriage. Profit is critical in all transactions: the financials and EBITDA, a recast P&L, and opportunities to gain scale by eliminating redundancy are all part of the equation. But the wise entrepreneur recognizes that their business, when merged with another, must sync up culturally.

I've found in most mergers that there is still one acquiring and another being acquired. You just need to recognize which one you are and the implications that follow. When people use the term "merger," they are most likely saving the feelings and ego of the business being absorbed and acquired by the other. There may be key elements that the acquiree brings to the table that will replace the acquirer's system, process, or people; however, it is naive to believe that this financial transaction doesn't come without expectations.

In saying this, I do not mean to imply that mergers (or the word itself) are a bad thing. What I am trying to communicate is that when you have more transparency around what's actually happening, people can manage their expectations as they go through the process. Either way, as an industry consolidates, there is tremendous potential for both parties as competition and scarcity play into the business's ability to thrive. Whether merger, acquisition, consolidation, or something else, the opportunity to take 1 and 1 and make 11—that's potential. That is quantum growth!

The Better Entrepreneur will read this chapter and see that the opportunity comes from recognizing that the problems they face are simply more potential for growth. The opportunity to reinvent, do something new, or enhance what already works can be invigorating. Decades of experience show that it is up to the entrepreneur to see and capture potential. That is how your business started, and that is the lifeblood of what will take it into the next stage. You must see it and surround yourself with those who can help you to seize it. The culmination of the 5Ps is their symbiotic nature; each principle unlocks the next layer of potential. Potential is what you pass to the next generation, and it is there that your legacy continues. If it is immortality that you seek, lead to the potential, and you'll not be disappointed.

WHAT'S YOUR BETTER?

A*ct boldly, and unseen forces will come to your aid.* Never have these words resonated more strongly with me than when I started our consulting business almost ten years ago. If you recall, my entrepreneurial experience began more than twenty years ago and was a spectacular failure. I was in my mid-twenties and didn't understand much about business, even with a bachelor's degree in business management. The stuff you learn in college can only get you so far. I wasn't smart enough to seek mentorship or advice from someone with more experience.

The axiom is irrefutable: "If you want to go fast, go alone; if you want to go far, go together." Well, my friend, I went fast, and the burnout was instant and glorious. Within six months, I was out of cash, had been swindled by a strategic partner, closed shop, and suffered some severe financial woes. There is wisdom in realizing that there is opposition in all things. That wisdom was all I had to grasp onto in some of my darkest and most humiliating hours.

PAIN, DISAPPOINTMENT, AND FAILURE

The crucible of self-reflection when you've failed is absolutely brutal. The self-doubt, self-loathing, and hit to your self-worth will rock you to your core. The failure of a business is something no one wants to go through. It took me over a decade to try again.

Now, that having been said, the behavior is self-evident on the basis of the description. Many of us are inclined to focus on ourselves, wallow in self-pity, and spiral in the echo chamber. I've referred to this experience (stealing the term from a mentor) as "the purple funk." It's the time we spend in our mental space, bouncing back and forth between the left wall of emotion and the right wall of thoughts, the negative on one hand that's feeding the negative on the other, and down further and further we go into the abyss of the purple funk.

There are only a few methods to pull yourself out of that purple funk, and all of them are externally focused. For us to move forward and upward, we must focus outward and break through the suffocating self-loathing.

Michael Jordan once responded to an interview question about his success with, "I have failed over and over in my life, and that is why I succeed." In my recollection, I cannot think of, in all the annals of history, any great human story that has not been fraught with pain, disappointment, and failure. The ultimate success may vary, but the common theme that we love and respect is the individual's ability to fail, get back up, and succeed.

In writing this, I hope to communicate to any reader currently in a state of "failure" that there's real value in keeping your feet moving. Your business may fail, your financial situation may be in ruins, and all hope may feel lost, but your story doesn't end here, unless you decide it does.

It might seem odd that I've started the end of this book talking about failure, and perhaps it is. The best entrepreneurs I've worked with have all failed to some extent. What I admire most in these failures is the lonely step each of them took into the dark, the unknown. They made the ultimate bet: on themselves and their purpose, passion, or cause. The successful entrepreneur is willing to risk their future by placing that risk on their own abilities and tenacious work.

As I stated at the beginning of the book, entrepreneurship is a calling. It is not for everyone. The safety of a steady paycheck and the sense of security that comes from being an employee of a Fortune 500 company are great comforts. In fact, there are billions of us who have chosen that path, and for many, it is the right path.

THE E-MYTH

As we reviewed in the Purpose Principle chapter, understanding who you are is a critical element of your ability to be successful. Self-reflection and awareness, and perhaps some wise counsel from those around you, can give you the needed information to determine whether you're an intrapreneur or an entrepreneur.

If the desire is there, it may not be enough. Case in point: Several of the business owners we coach never actually intended to be the CEO. They simply got on a path where they were great as technicians; they created a very high-paying job built on their unique abilities. They grew a clientele and found that they needed an assistant. Then they needed more help. Eventually, they woke up with ten, then twenty or more, people on the team. All these people had needs and wants, and the original high-paying job had become a full-fledged enterprise.

As described by Michael E. Gerber in *The E-Myth*, the technician added two additional hats (the manager and the entrepreneur) over time. And for many, they are not interested in anything beyond the technician role. The best move for people in this situation is to hire someone for the other roles or pursue a strategic merger with a company that already has this skill set in place. Forcing yourself into something you don't have a passion for or the skillset for is a very challenging way to live. Being true to oneself is one of the most important lessons those with fewer years ahead of them than behind them will tell you.

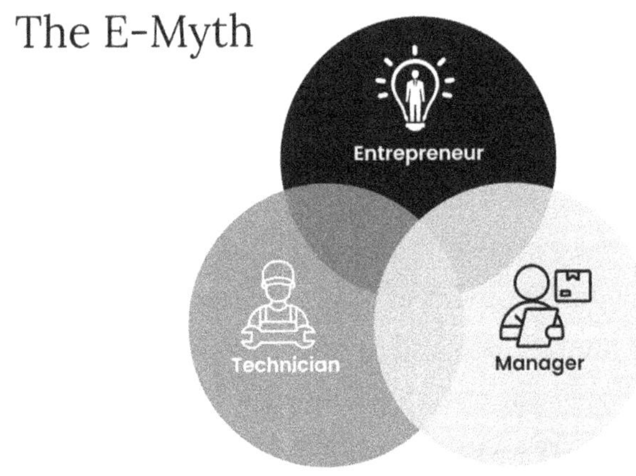

If you have the desire and are willing to put in the work to build the skillset, this can be a worthy use of your time. It can become your new purpose, cause, or passion. It can be the fuel that reignites you for the next chapter. If this is the desired outcome and you want to go from technician to entrepreneur, you must prepare yourself to make the transition. Education and knowledge can bring the wisdom you need to make the leap.

While grit and hard work are crucial to the successful entrepreneur, IQ (intelligence quotient) and CQ (curiosity quotient) are equally valuable. Many business owners are naturally able to wield their power with charisma and tenacity. The better entrepreneur builds on that charisma and tenacity and gets the mentorship required to be effective in application and in title. Too many times, there is a self-declaration as the entrepreneur without the preparation or know-how.

It has been said that you should surround yourself with people who push you, people who might be smarter and even have greater faith in you than you do yourself. I have found that in my wife, Kim. She is a key contributor who gave me the push I needed to begin my side hustle. We knew that I had a desire, at some point in the future, to begin a coaching and consulting business. I was distracted by the whirlwind and, frankly, a bit in my comfort zone of "just doing my job" to the best of my abilities and seeing success in the business I was serving. It felt good, it was safe, and it provided a solid salary (if not a truly fulfilling one).

With a bit of financial strain but even more motivation, I had a greater calling. Kim reminded me of the need to fulfill the promises I had made to myself. May you be fortunate enough in your entrepreneurial journey to find your "Kim." The person who believes in you sees what you aren't seeing, they're willing to pray for and with you, and they are bold enough to challenge you to do and to be better! If you don't have that, you must find it.

There are moments in your life that you can reflect on: switch points where the train rails move three inches in one direction, and the train and its payload are sent on a completely different path. These crucial conversations are destiny-forming.

Beginning the process by having the conversation with my boss was that switch point. I was greatly blessed with an incredibly supportive boss, and her willingness to entertain this new venture was a key element of my ability to take the step. She didn't create an either-or scenario, and for this, I will always be grateful.

RISK MITIGATION

Great preparation leads to great outcomes. If you have a switch-point conversation that needs to happen, put the time in, do your due diligence, and have the conversation.

The best entrepreneurs I've worked with act boldly. They realize there's risk and put in the preparation to mitigate it. If you have the ability to start your side hustle with the support of your current employer, that is the ideal situation to be in. Be strategic in how you approach the connections and opportunities in your life. Too many entrepreneurs miss the mark by being underprepared or unaware of the significance of a crucial conversation.

The best entrepreneurs I've worked with act boldly. They realize there's risk and put in the preparation to mitigate it.

Once the journey has been decided upon—or perhaps you're already well into it—the 5Ps are the fundamental components of how successful entrepreneurs achieve great results. As we have coached leadership teams on how to effectively execute on their Purpose, People, Process, Profit, and Potential, our experience in seeing better teams, better businesses, and better freedom has been fulfilling and meaningful.

You gain real traction and solve the right problems at the right time when you can name the problems, challenges, and issues in your business and organize them in a way that can be digested by the entire team. In a sense, you're upgrading your problems. Every business has and will always have its issues and challenges. The zen comes when you have a way to articulate what the problem is, prioritize its urgency, and solve it at the right time.

A common piece of feedback I've received when onboarding new coaching clients is how this approach is not only revelatory but also revolutionary. When you hear that what you've worked on in the first month of an engagement is more than the entrepreneur accomplished in an entire year's worth of work with a previous coach, that's powerful.

Whether you're a staunch DIYer who would never pay for a coach or someone who's had multiple coaches help them build their business all along, I hope this content will simply be of value in whatever manner is best for you.

So, what's next for you?

I've provided some of my favorite quotes on the idea of execution in the following pages. Any internet search will give you the same or similar results, I'm sure. The point of putting these in front of you as we wrap up this journey together is to remind you of the critical nature of implementation.

I've found myself having read hundreds of books over my lifetime, many with great ideas, tips, and innovations. They've expanded my mind, opened my way of thinking, and have been incredibly valuable. What I've found even more lasting are the actions I've taken and the books that have given me the tools necessary to do something with their content.

That is the intention of this book. I've organized my thoughts into these principles, and the QR codes leading to tools, content, and next steps are designed to help you take action.

An entrepreneur's world is chaotic at times. There are many competing pressures, tasks, and priorities to attend to. Ironically, the term "priority," in its original Latin, was never intended to be pluralized. Yet in our modern-day wisdom, we felt we could improve and set unrealistic expectations: multiple priorities!

GOOD, BETTER, BEST

The irony of all of this is that many of the actions you may be taking are good by nature and design. They benefit the business, your customers or clients, and your future. The lens that has served me well comes from the wise words of Dallin Oaks, former Utah Supreme Court Justice, who recommends categorizing your choices into Good, Better, and Best.

Consider a day filled with a myriad of options. Ask yourself: *Is what you're doing now a good use of your time? Is there something better? In the end, what is the best use of my time, talents, and resources in this exact moment?*

With this view of any given day, you can become more conscious and aware of the actions you're taking. Everyone can be busy, everyone can be productive, but the highest and best use of your energy and talent is the epitome of achieving your purpose.

I did a podcast in 2025 with a friend, Brian Bosley. He's hosted this podcast for the past several years with great success. During our conversation, we talked about the question, "Why are you here?" Finding that purpose is not only meaningful, but if you believe in its value, it is an imperative.

As you contemplate the next steps to take, I ask you to consider not only "Why are you here?" but "Why are you here *now*?" Consider your purpose in the here and now.

Is the action you're taking truly important? Are you falling prey to the comfort and ease of being busy or doing what is familiar—or, even worse, allowing your environment to act upon you, rather than you acting upon it?

You must break the cycle if you are to achieve your best use, to become the ideal, and to live in the ideal for as long as possible.

So, when I ask what's next for you, be thoughtful, and take the words of wisdom and actionable items outlined in this book—and go forth and achieve!

Here are the quotes to get you into the right mindset:

"A good plan violently executed now is better than a perfect plan executed next week."
— George S. Patton

"Execution is a systematic process of rigorously discussing hows and whats, questioning, tenaciously following through, and ensuring accountability."
— Larry Bossidy

"Ideas are easy. Execution is everything. It takes a team to win."
— John Doerr

"Success doesn't necessarily come from breakthrough innovation but from flawless execution."
— Naveen Jain

"The best strategy is useless if it is not executed well."
— Roberto Goizueta

"No matter how brilliant the strategy, it's worth nothing unless it's implemented properly."
— Mark Fields

"Vision without execution is just another word for hallucination."
— Mark Hurd

"Do not reveal what you have thought upon doing, but by wise counsel keep it secret, being determined to carry it into execution."
— Chanakya

Lastly, thanks for being my companion along this journey. I've been meaning to write this book for some time, and it has been liberating and gratifying to finally work on it.

"The path to frustration, disappointment, and a personal living hell is paved with good intentions."

My recommendation for you from here:

- Be the Human God Intended You to Be.
- Act Boldly, and Unseen Forces Will Come to Your Aid.
- Live the Life You Want NOW.

ABOUT THE AUTHOR

JT Wiederholt is the founder of Balance Approach, a leadership coaching and consulting firm dedicated to helping entrepreneurs and organizations unlock their full potential. A seasoned entrepreneur himself, JT is a Certified Financial Planner® with a master's degree in Financial Planning, and serves as a partner in a successful wealth management firm. He brings a background of corporate sales, leadership, and executive experience. Married for nearly thirty years and a proud father of six children—one in heaven—he grounds his professional work in the values of family and resilience. An avid reader and passionate traveler, JT has explored more than seventy countries (and counting), drawing inspiration from diverse cultures and perspectives. With a blend of personal experience and professional expertise, he equips entrepreneurs and executives to build businesses that thrive with purpose and lasting impact.

REFERENCES

Bandura, Albert. *Social Learning Theory.* Englewood Cliffs, NJ: Prentice-Hall, 1977.

Bureau of Labor Statistics. "Business Employment Dynamics: Establishment Age and Survival Data." U.S. Department of Labor. Accessed [date of access]. https://www.bls.gov/bdm.

Christensen, Clayton M. *How Will You Measure Your Life?* New York: Harper Business, 2012.

Collins, Jim. *Good to Great: Why Some Companies Make the Leap... and Others Don't.* New York: HarperBusiness, 2001.

Drucker Institute. "About Peter Drucker and the Drucker Institute." Accessed November 4, 2025. https://www.drucker.institute/.

Edmondson, Amy C. *The Fearless Organization: Creating Psychological Safety in the Workplace for Learning, Innovation, and Growth.* Hoboken, NJ: Wiley, 2019.

Emerson, Ralph Waldo. "Your actions speak so loudly, I cannot hear what you are saying." Quotation attributed to Emerson; original publication date unknown.

Exit Planning Institute. "State of Owner Readiness: 2013 Survey Results." Cleveland, OH: Exit Planning Institute, 2013.

Fischer, James. *Navigating the Growth Curve: 9 Stages of Entrepreneurial Success.* Minneapolis, MN: Business Ferret Press, 2006.

Gallup. "State of the Global Workplace: 2021 Report." Washington, DC: Gallup Press, 2021.

Gerber, Michael E. *The E-Myth Revisited: Why Most Small Businesses Don't Work and What to Do about It.* New York: HarperBusiness, 1995.

Gladwell, Malcolm. *Outliers: The Story of Success.* New York: Little, Brown and Company, 2008.

Goleman, Daniel. *Emotional Intelligence: Why It Can Matter More Than IQ.* New York: Bantam Books, 1995.

Goleman, Daniel, Richard E. Boyatzis, and Annie McKee. *Primal Leadership: Unleashing the Power of Emotional Intelligence.* Boston: Harvard Business Review Press, 2013.

Kouzes, James M., and Barry Z. Posner. *The Leadership Challenge: How to Make Extraordinary Things Happen in Organizations.* 6th ed. Hoboken, NJ: Wiley, 2017.

Lencioni, Patrick. *The Five Dysfunctions of a Team: A Leadership Fable.* San Francisco: Jossey-Bass, 2002.

Maxwell, John C. *Developing the Leader Within You 2.0.* Nashville, TN: HarperCollins Leadership, 2018.

McGregor, Douglas. *The Human Side of Enterprise.* New York: McGraw-Hill, 1960.

Northouse, Peter G. *Leadership: Theory and Practice.* 9th ed. Thousand Oaks, CA: SAGE Publications, 2021.

Rock, David, and Jeffrey Schwartz. "The Neuroscience of Leadership" *strategy+business.* Issue 43, Summer 2006. https://www.strategy-business.com/media/file/sb43_06207.pdf?origin=publication_detail.

Sinek, Simon. *Leaders Eat Last: Why Some Teams Pull Together and Others Don't.* New York: Portfolio Penguin, 2014.

Think2Perform. "Values Exercise." Accessed November 4, 2025. https://www.think2perform.com/values.

Thoreau, Henry David. "For every thousand hacking at the leaves of evil, there is one striking at the root." In *A Week on the Concord and Merrimack Rivers.* 1863.

Wickman, Gino. *Traction: Get a Grip on Your Business.* Dallas, TX: BenBella Books, 2012.

THANK YOU FOR READING MY BOOK!

Download Your Free Gifts

Just to say thanks for buying and reading my book, I would like to give you a few free bonus gifts, no strings attached!

To Download Now, Visit:

I appreciate your interest in my book and value your feedback as it helps me improve future versions of this book. I would appreciate it if you could leave your invaluable review on Amazon.com with your feedback. Thank you!

www.ingramcontent.com/pod-product-compliance
Lightning Source LLC
Chambersburg PA
CBHW031403180326
41458CB00043B/6590/J
* 9 7 8 1 9 6 9 3 7 2 8 5 8 *